THE WRITE STUFF

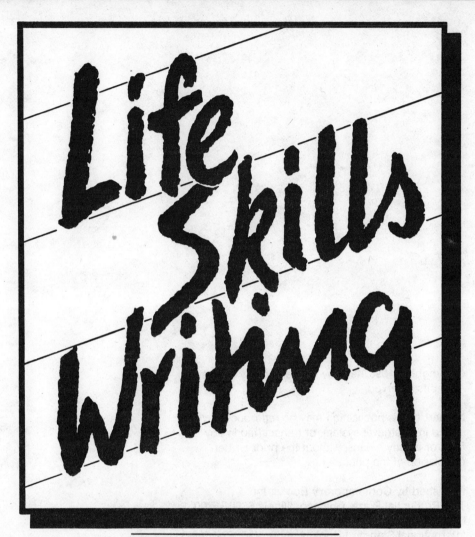

Life Skills Writing

Exercise Book

Project Editor—*Karin Evans*

CB
CONTEMPORARY
BOOKS
CHICAGO

Published by Contemporary Books, Inc.
Two Prudential Plaza, Chicago, Illinois 60601-6790
Manufactured in the United States of America
International Standard Book Number: 0-8092-5099-3

Published simultaneously in Canada by
Fitzhenry & Whiteside
195 Allstate Parkway
Markham, Ontario L3R 4T8
Canada

Editorial
Julie Landau
Mark Boone
Christine M. Benton

Editorial Director
Caren Van Slyke

Production Editor
J. D. Fairbanks

Art and Illustrations
Princess Louise El
Lisa Knopf
Rosemary Morrisey-Herzberg

Typography
Lisa Waitrovich

Cover Design
Robb Pawlak

Contents

TO THE STUDENT

Life in America today is more complicated than it used to be. You can't go through life easily without being able to write. The ability to write doesn't mean just being able to sign your name. Nor does it mean being able to write a novel. Rather, it means being able to write well enough to complete many everyday tasks. In some situations this ability can spell the difference between success and failure. Some basic writing tasks include:

★ filling out forms
★ writing instructions and messages
★ writing letters
★ writing to express your opinion

The Write Stuff Life Skills Exercise Book focuses on writing tasks such as these, tasks encountered in people's daily lives.

This workbook follows a modern family whose lives bring them face to face with situations in which they need to write. You will get the chance to practice your writing skills along with them as they cope with these situations.

As a result of completing this workbook, you should have increased confidence in your ability to handle common writing tasks. But before you get started, meet the Hunter family.

knopf

Paul Hunter, 44, and his wife, Mercedes, 42, have been married for 19 years. They have three children: Ramon, 18; Rita, 15; and Paula, 8. Like many marriages, the Hunters' has had its ups and downs. But now the relationship has hit rock bottom.

Paul, a foreman, was just one week short of marking his 25th year with Hoosier Steel Works of Indiana when the plant shut down and he was thrown out of work. He had never worked anywhere else.

Mercedes had seen it coming for several years: first the reduced working hours, then the cutback in wage increases, finally the layoffs. Paul didn't look for another job because he believed the plant would recover.

During this time, Mercedes had tried to persuade him to move to San Antonio. She was sure he'd find work there. Paul wouldn't go. He thought Mercedes just wanted to be near her family so that they could meddle in his family's business.

After the plant closed, Paul refused to seek work. He sat around the house, wallowing in self-pity. Within a year, the Hunter household became a war zone. The two girls grew afraid of their grouchy father, but Ramon constantly defied him. Mercedes, backed by Ramon, complained often. She sometimes reverted to her native tongue, a habit that angered Paul all the more because he couldn't understand Spanish.

Paul repeatedly threatened to leave for California, where he had friends. One day he made good on his threat and took a Greyhound bus to California. He left behind a stack of unpaid bills and the broken-down family car.

Mercedes reacted without emotion when she found out that he'd left. She wrote a letter to her mother in San Antonio to tell her what had happened. One week later, Juanita Esperanza appeared on Mercedes's doorstep, carrying two straw satchels and wearing the pair of huaraches Mercedes had sent her for Christmas.

Juanita had come to live with Mercedes and help manage the household. Mercedes was faced with the tasks of orienting her mother to the new environment and finding a job to support the family.

In this book, you will sometimes see references to two other books in Contemporary's "The Write Stuff" series, *Putting It in Paragraphs* and *Writing for a Purpose*. These books can give your more practice and information about writing.

CHAPTER 1

FILLING IN THE BLANKS

Filling out forms completely and correctly will be very important for Mercedes and Paul as they go their separate ways—and for their children too. They will need to be able to fill out everyday forms like checks and deposit slips. In addition, the changes they are facing may require them to fill out even more forms—such as voter registration and W-4 (withholding tax) forms.

Forms may seem picky and insignificant compared to some of the more exciting things we do. But all this "red tape" gives you access to the money you have in the bank, government services such as social security, and privileges such as voting.

Forms can be long or short, simple or complicated. Some may seem utterly impossible. Use the following guidelines for filling out forms as you study and practice the forms in this chapter.

GUIDELINES FOR FILLING OUT FORMS

Before You Begin—

1. Read through the entire form first—*before* you fill in any part of it.
2. If there are instructions, read them all the way through, referring back to the form to be sure you understand each part.
3. If you have questions, ask a knowledgeable person for assistance before you begin to fill out the form. Go back to the person who gave you the form. If you took the form home with you, call the place where you got it. Some forms, like income tax forms, give you a phone number to call if you need assistance.

As You Fill Out the Form—

4. Fill in every space. If a question doesn't apply to you, put a line through the space (——), or write *NA*, an abbreviation meaning "Not Applicable."
5. Give complete and accurate information.
6. When you're done, go back and read over the completed form to check for errors and make sure you didn't overlook any part.

BANKING FORMS

Mercedes handles the money for her family of five. She makes deposits into their checking and savings accounts and writes checks to pay the bills.

FILLING OUT CHECKING ACCOUNT DEPOSIT SLIPS

Last week Mercedes deposited three checks into her checking account. The checks were for $239.45, $64.38, and $10.00. She wanted $30.00 back in cash for groceries. Study the filled-out deposit slip that shows her transaction. Pay special attention to the following important details:

1. The blank line below the date is for a signature.
2. The back side of the deposit slip is used only when there are too many checks to list on the front.
3. *Less cash received* is the amount of cash Mercedes wants to take with her after she has deposited the checks.
4. The amount of the *net deposit* is the total of the checks minus the amount of cash Mercedes wants to take with her.

DEPOSIT TICKET

MERCEDES HUNTER
9333 S. ELKHART AVE.
PORTAGE, IN 47314

DATE *February 5* 19 *90*

Mercedes Hunter

DELUXE National State Bank
Your City, U.S.A. 12345

⑆⑆:2345⑈6789⑆: 12345678⑈ 20

	CASH	—	
CHECKS		239	45
		64	38
		10	00
TOTAL FROM OTHER SIDE		—	
TOTAL		313	83
LESS CASH RECEIVED		30	00
NET DEPOSIT		283	83

USE OTHER SIDE FOR ADDITIONAL LISTING

70-2422
719
Checks and other items are received for deposit subject to the terms and conditions of this bank's collection agreement.

BE SURE EACH ITEM IS PROPERLY ENDORSED

Exercise A: Check Your Understanding

Based on Mercedes's deposit slip above, answer the following questions in the blanks provided.

1. Why did Mercedes put a line through the top blank next to

   *CASH?*_____

2. Fill in the numbers that show how Mercedes calculated her net deposit:

   _____ – _____ = _____

3. If Mercedes had more than three checks to deposit, where would she

   write the amounts of the additional checks?_____

Answers are on page 88.

7

Exercise B: Filling out a Checking Account Deposit Slip

This week Mercedes has two checks to deposit. The amounts of the checks are $75.16 and $2.67. She would like $20.00 back in cash. Fill out her deposit slip for her. Check your work against the example on page 7.

```
        ┌─────────────────────────┐          ┌──────────────────────────┐
        │     DEPOSIT TICKET      │          │ C      CASH              │
        │                         │          │ H                        │
        │   MERCEDES HUNTER       │          │ E                        │
        │   9333 S. ELKHART AVE.  │          │ C                        │
        │   PORTAGE, IN 47314     │          │ K                        │
        │                         │          │ S  TOTAL FROM OTHER SIDE │
        │ DATE_____19____  │          │      TOTAL               │
        │                         │      ➡   │    LESS CASH RECEIVED    │
        │ _____   │          │      NET DEPOSIT         │
        │                         │          │ USE OTHER SIDE FOR ADDITIONAL LISTING
        │  DELUXE National State Bank
        │   Your City, U.S.A. 12345
```

70-2422
719

Checks and other items are received for deposit subject to the terms and conditions of this bank's collection agreement.

BE SURE EACH ITEM IS PROPERLY ENDORSED

⑆⑈2345⑈6789⑇ 12345678⑈ 20

WRITING CHECKS

Mercedes has received a bill that she must pay. She will write a check for $23.78 to Sears, Roebuck & Co. Study her check below, paying special attention to the following important details:

1. The amount of the check is written entirely in numerals on the right side of the check: *$23.78*.
2. The name of the receiver of the check is written on the line that begins *Pay to the order of.*
3. Underneath the name of the receiver of the check, the amount is written again. This time the number of whole dollars is written in words, *twenty-three*, followed by a fraction that tells the number of cents out of a hundred that are left, or *78/100*.
4. Checks must be signed in the lower right corner by an authorized person.
5. Next to *memo* you can write anything that will help you or the receiver remember what the payment is for. You can also leave this line blank.

Exercise C: Practice Writing Checks

Write checks to pay the rest of Mercedes's bills for this week:

    1. $44.17 to Columbus Power and Light Co. on Feb. 12, 1990

    2. $30.00 to Dr. Susannah Pirotti, D.D.S., on Feb. 13, 1990

Check your work against the example on page 8.

REGISTERING TO VOTE

Soon after Paul's arrival in California, he became interested in local politics. Watching politicians campaigning for office reminded him that in a few months he would want to vote. He knew he needed to register to vote in his new state.

To register to vote, you need several pieces of identification. Usually a driver's license or state ID card, checks or a bill showing your current address, and one other form of identification will do. Be sure all the addresses on your identification are current.

If you're not sure where to register, call or visit your city hall. Also, public libraries often register voters, as do many political organizations.

A voter registration form looks a little more complicated than a check or a deposit slip, but it is not hard to fill out. There are a few words and phrases on the form that you might not know. If you need to, use a dictionary. However, if you read the form carefully, you may be able to figure out the meanings of unfamiliar words or phrases from their context.

Exercise D: Filling Out Paul's Voter Registration Form

Use the information about Paul listed below and the hints on page 6 to fill out this form. Read over the entire form before you begin.

Mr. Paul Hunter

residence and mailing address: 3421 N. Grove Ave., Apt. 5
                               Los Angeles, 92106

county: Los Angeles

telephone: 213-555-0075

intersection of Grove Ave. and Dodge St.

member of Democratic Party

born Dec. 21, 1946, in Illinois

unemployed

Social Security Number: 123-45-6789

not currently registered to vote in California

PRINT IN INK—ESCRIBA EN LETRA DE MOLDE EN TINTA

STATE OF—ESTADO DE CALIFORNIA
COUNTY OF—CONDADO DE LOS ANGELES

AFFIDAVIT OF REGISTRATION—DECLARACIÓN JURADA DE EMPADRONAMIENTO

1 Optional - Opcional— ☐ Mr/Sr ☐ Mrs/Sra ☐ Miss/Srta ☐ Ms Name - Nombre (first - nombre) (middle - segundo) (last - apellido)	**WARNING:** Perjury is punishable by imprisonment in State prison of not less than 1 nor more than 14 yrs. § 126 Penal Code, 2015.5 Civil Proc. — **AVISO** – El juramento en falso es castigable con encarcelamiento en la prisión del estado por no menos de uno y no más de catorce años. § 126 Penal Code, 2015.5 Civ. Proc.
2 Residence - Domicilio (No.) (Street - Calle) (Apt. No. - Núm. del Apt.)	I am a citizen of the United States and will be at least 18 years of age at the time of the next election. I am not imprisoned or on parole for the conviction of a felony which disqualifies me from voting. I certify under penalty of perjury that the information on this affidavit is true and correct. — Soy ciudadano de los Estados Unidos y tendré por lo menos 18 años de edad para la próxima elección. No estoy preso o bajo el régimen de libertad provisional por un crimen que me prive del derecho de votar. Juro bajo pena de falso juramento que la información en esta Declaración Jurada es verdadera y correcta.
3 City - Ciudad **4** Zip Code - Zona Postal	
5 Describe location of residence: (cross streets, section, township, range) - Describa la localidad de su residencia: (Calles que atraviesan, etc.)	**13** Signature – Firma
6 Mailing Address (if different) - Dirección Postal (si diferente) (Rte or Box)	Date – Fecha Subscribed in County of – Firmada en Condado de
City - Ciudad Zip Code - Zona Postal	**14** Signature person assisting (if any) – Firma, persona que ayuda (Si hubiera)
7 Political Party - Partido Político (Check One - Indique uno) ☐ American Independent ☐ Democratic ☐ Peace and Freedom ☐ Republican ☐ Decline to State - Se niega a declarar ☐ Other - Otro _____	Date - Fecha **15** ☐ I will require assistance at the polls ☐ Yo necesito ayuda en la caseta de votación
8 Date of Birth / Fecha de nacimiento **9** State or Country of Birth / Estado o país de nacimiento mo - mes / day - día / yr - año	**PRIOR REGISTRATION PORTION: PORCIÓN DE EMPADRONAMIENTO PREVIOS** ARE YOU CURRENTLY REGISTERED TO VOTE IN CALIFORNIA? ☐ NO / ¿ESTA UD. EMPADRONADO PARA VOTAR ACTUALMENTE EN CALIFORNIA? ☐ YES - Si (If YES, fill in below - Si afirmativo, llene los espacios abajo)
10 Occupation - Profesión u Oficio	NAME AS PREVIOUSLY REGISTERED - NOMBRE COMO PREVIAMENTE EMPADRONADO
11 Telephone (Optional) / Teléfono (Opcional) Social Security No. (Optional) / Núm. de segura social (Opcional)	Former Address – Dirección Anterior:
	City – Ciudad County – Condado
12 ☐ I prefer election materials in English ☐ Prefiero materiales electorales en español	Political Party – Partido Político **ZA 726149**
	Office Use

The filled-out form is on page 88.

W-4 WITHHOLDING ALLOWANCE CERTIFICATE

Mercedes and Paul are now searching for jobs. When they become employed, one of the first things they will do for their new employers will be to fill out a W-4 form. The purpose of this form is to tell the employer how much money should be deducted from a person's paycheck for federal income taxes.

The W-4 form is not a long form, but it has many important instructions. It also has two parts—the main form and a worksheet that helps you figure out information you need for the main form.

In the exercise that follows, you will fill out a W-4 form for yourself. Be sure to use the hints on page 6 to help you. In particular, be sure to read all the instructions before you begin.

Exercise E: Filling Out Your W-4 Form

Fill out the following form as though you were just starting your present job. If you do not work, make up any details you need. Starting in the second column, instructions A–E refer to the worksheet on page 13.

19**90** Form W-4

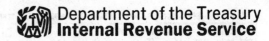

**Department of the Treasury
Internal Revenue Service**

Purpose. Complete Form W-4 so that your employer can withhold the correct amount of Federal income tax from your pay.

Exemption From Withholding. Read line 6 of the certificate below to see if you can claim exempt status. *If exempt, complete line 6; but do not complete lines 4 and 5.* No Federal income tax will be withheld from your pay. This exemption expires February 15, 1991.

Basic Instructions. Employees who are not exempt should complete the Personal Allowances Worksheet. Additional worksheets are provided on page 2 for employees to adjust their withholding allowances based on itemized deductions, adjustments to income, or two-earner/two-job situations. Complete all worksheets that apply to your situation. The worksheets will help you figure the number of withholding allowances you are

entitled to claim. However, you may claim fewer allowances than this.

Head of Household. Generally, you may claim head of household filing status on your tax return only if you are unmarried and pay more than 50% of the costs of keeping up a home for yourself and your dependent(s) or other qualifying individuals.

Nonwage Income. If you have a large amount of nonwage income, such as interest or dividends, you should consider making estimated tax payments using Form 1040-ES. Otherwise, you may find that you owe additional tax at the end of the year.

Two-Earner/Two-Jobs. If you have a working spouse or more than one job, figure the total number of allowances you are entitled to claim on all jobs using worksheets from only one Form

W-4. This total should be divided among all jobs. Your withholding will usually be most accurate when all allowances are claimed on the W-4 filed for the highest paying job and zero allowances are claimed for the others.

Advance Earned Income Credit. If you are eligible for this credit, you can receive it added to your paycheck throughout the year. For details, obtain Form W-5 from your employer.

Check Your Withholding. After your W-4 takes effect, you can use **Publication 919,** Is My Withholding Correct for 1990?, to see how the dollar amount you are having withheld compares to your estimated total annual tax. Call 1-800-424-3676 (in Hawaii and Alaska, check your local telephone directory) to order this publication. Check your local telephone directory for the IRS assistance number if you need further help.

Personal Allowances Worksheet

A Enter "1" for **yourself** if no one else can claim you as a dependent . . . . **A** _____

B Enter "1" if:
  1. You are single and have only one job; or
  2. You are married, have only one job, and your spouse does not work; or
  3. Your wages from a second job or your spouse's wages (or the total of both) are $2,500 or less.
  . . . . **B** _____

C Enter "1" for your **spouse.** But, you may choose to enter "0" if you are married and have either a working spouse or more than one job (this may help you avoid having too little tax withheld) . . . . **C** _____

D Enter number of **dependents** (other than your spouse or yourself) whom you will claim on your tax return . . . . **D** _____

E Enter "1" if you will file as a **head of household** on your tax return (see conditions under "Head of Household," above) . . **E** _____

F Enter "1" if you have at least $1,500 of **child or dependent care expenses** for which you plan to claim a credit . . . . **F** _____

G Add lines A through F and enter total here . . . . ▶ **G** _____

For accuracy, do all worksheets that apply.
- If you plan to **itemize or claim adjustments to income** and want to reduce your withholding, turn to the Deductions and Adjustments Worksheet on page 2.
- If you are **single** and have **more than one job** and your combined earnings from all jobs exceed $25,000 OR if you are **married** and have a **working spouse or more than one job,** and the combined earnings from all jobs exceed $44,000, then turn to the Two-Earner/Two-Job Worksheet on page 2 if you want to avoid having too little tax withheld.
- If **neither** of the above situations applies to you, **stop here** and enter the number from line G on line 4 of Form W-4 below.

-------------------- Cut here and give the certificate to your employer. Keep the top portion for your records. --------------------

Form **W-4**
Department of the Treasury
Internal Revenue Service

Employee's Withholding Allowance Certificate

▶ **For Privacy Act and Paperwork Reduction Act Notice, see reverse.**

OMB No. 1545-0010

19**90**

1 Type or print your first name and middle initial	Last name	2 Your social security number

Home address (number and street or rural route)	3 Marital status	☐ Single ☐ Married
City or town, state, and ZIP code		☐ Married, but withhold at higher Single rate. **Note:** *If married, but legally separated, or spouse is a nonresident alien, check the Single box.*

4 Total number of allowances you are claiming (from line G above or from the Worksheets on back if they apply) . . . **4** ____

5 Additional amount, if any, you want deducted from each pay . . . . **5** $ ____

6 I claim exemption from withholding and I certify that I meet **ALL** of the following conditions for exemption:
  - Last year I had a right to a refund of **ALL** Federal income tax withheld because I had **NO** tax liability; **AND**
  - This year I expect a refund of **ALL** Federal income tax withheld because I expect to have **NO** tax liability; **AND**
  - This year if my income exceeds $500 and includes nonwage income, another person cannot claim me as a dependent.

If you meet all of the above conditions, enter the year effective and "EXEMPT" here . . . . ▶ **6** | 19 ____

7 Are you a full-time student? (**Note:** *Full-time students are not automatically exempt.*) . . . . **7** ☐ Yes ☐ No

Under penalties of perjury, I certify that I am entitled to the number of withholding allowances claimed on this certificate or entitled to claim exempt status.

Employee's signature ▶ _____ Date ▶ _____ , 19 ____

8 Employer's name and address (**Employer:** Complete 8 and 10 **only if sending to IRS**)	9 Office code (optional)	10 Employer identification number

Deductions and Adjustments Worksheet

Note: *Use this worksheet only if you plan to itemize deductions or claim adjustments to income on your 1990 tax return.*

1 Enter an estimate of your 1990 itemized deductions. These include: qualifying home mortgage interest, 10% of personal interest, charitable contributions, state and local taxes (but not sales taxes), medical expenses in excess of 7.5% of your income, and miscellaneous deductions (most miscellaneous deductions are now deductible only in excess of 2% of your income) . . . . **1** $ _____

2 Enter: { $5,450 if married filing jointly or qualifying widow(er)
           $4,750 if head of household
           $3,250 if single
           $2,725 if married filing separately } . . . . **2** $ _____

3 **Subtract** line 2 from line 1. If line 2 is greater than line 1, enter zero . . . . **3** $ _____

4 Enter an estimate of your 1990 adjustments to income. These include alimony paid and deductible IRA contributions . . **4** $ _____

5 **Add** lines 3 and 4 and enter the total . . . . **5** $ _____

6 Enter an estimate of your 1990 nonwage income (such as dividends or interest income) . . . . **6** $ _____

7 **Subtract** line 6 from line 5. Enter the result, but not less than zero . . . . **7** $ _____

8 **Divide** the amount on line 7 by $2,000 and enter the result here. Drop any fraction . . . **8** _____

9 Enter the number from Personal Allowances Worksheet, line G, on page 1 . . . . **9** _____

10 **Add** lines 8 and 9 and enter the total here. If you plan to use the Two-Earner/Two-Job Worksheet, also enter the total on line 1, below. Otherwise, **stop here** and enter this total on Form W-4, line 4 on page 1 . . . . . **10** _____

Two-Earner/Two-Job Worksheet

Note: *Use this worksheet only if the instructions at line G on page 1 direct you here.*

1 Enter the number from line G on page 1 (or from line 10 above if you used the Deductions and Adjustments Worksheet) . **1** _____

2 Find the number in **Table 1** below that applies to the **LOWEST** paying job and enter it here . . . . . **2** _____

3 If line 1 is **GREATER THAN OR EQUAL TO** line 2, subtract line 2 from line 1. Enter the result here (if zero, enter "0") and on Form W-4, line 4, on page 1. **DO NOT** use the rest of this worksheet . . . . **3** _____

Note: *If line 1 is LESS THAN line 2, enter "0" on Form W-4, line 4, on page 1. Complete lines 4–9 to calculate the additional dollar withholding necessary to avoid a year-end tax bill.*

4 Enter the number from line 2 of this worksheet . . . . **4** _____

5 Enter the number from line 1 of this worksheet . . . . **5** _____

6 **Subtract** line 5 from line 4 . . . . **6** _____

7 Find the amount in **Table 2** below that applies to the **HIGHEST** paying job and enter it here . . . . . . **7** $ _____

8 **Multiply** line 7 by line 6 and enter the result here. This is the additional annual withholding amount needed **8** $ _____

9 Divide line 8 by the number of pay periods each year. (For example, divide by 26 if you are paid every other week.) Enter the result here and on Form W-4, line 5, page 1. This is the additional amount to be withheld from each paycheck . . . . **9** $ _____

Table 1: Two-Earner/Two-Job Worksheet

Married Filing Jointly		All Others	
If wages from **LOWEST** paying job are—	Enter on line 2 above	If wages from **LOWEST** paying job are—	Enter on line 2 above
0 - $4,000	0	0 - $4,000	0
4,001 - 8,000	1	4,001 - 8,000	1
8,001 - 19,000	2	8,001 - 14,000	2
19,001 - 23,000	3	14,001 - 16,000	3
23,001 - 25,000	4	16,001 - 21,000	4
25,001 - 27,000	5	21,001 and over	5
27,001 - 29,000	6		
29,001 - 35,000	7		
35,001 - 41,000	8		
41,001 - 46,000	9		
46,001 and over	10		

Table 2: Two-Earner/Two-Job Worksheet

Married Filing Jointly		All Others	
If wages from **HIGHEST** paying job are—	Enter on line 7 above	If wages from **HIGHEST** paying job are—	Enter on line 7 above
0 - $44,000	$310	0 - $25,000	$310
44,001 - 90,000	570	25,001 - 52,000	570
90,001 and over	680	52,001 and over	680

Privacy Act and Paperwork Reduction Act Notice.—We ask for this information to carry out the Internal Revenue laws of the United States. We may give the information to the Department of Justice for civil or criminal litigation and to cities, states, and the District of Columbia for use in administering their tax laws. You are required to give this information to your employer.

The time needed to complete this form will vary depending on individual circumstances. The estimated average time is: **Recordkeeping 46 min.**, **Learning about the law or the form** 10 min., **Preparing the form** 70 min. If you have comments concerning the accuracy of these time estimates or suggestions for making this form more simple, we would be happy to hear from you. You can write to the **Internal Revenue Service**, Washington, DC 20224, Attn: IRS Reports Clearance Officer, T:FP; or the **Office of Management and Budget**, Paperwork Reduction Project (1545-0010), Washington, DC 20503.

★ U S GPO 1989-0-245-064

A filled-out W-4 form and worksheet are on page 89.

CHAPTER 2

INSTRUCTIONS, DIRECTIONS, AND MESSAGES

WRITING MESSAGES

When you write instructions, directions, and messages, you don't have to write in paragraphs or even complete sentences. However, your writing does have to make sense to the person you are writing to. In this lesson, you'll practice giving your reader complete and easy-to-follow information.

GUIDELINES FOR WRITING MESSAGES

When you write a message to someone, remember that you probably won't be there to explain it. Don't forget to:

1. Write the date at the top.
2. Address the note to a specific person.
3. Give complete information about everything that is relevant—times, locations, phone numbers, addresses.
4. Sign your name.

When Paul took off for California, he left this note for his children:

Model

MESSAGE

Feb. 1, 1990

Rita, Ramon, and Paula;

I'm going to live in California. I don't know where I'll be, but I'll get in touch with you when I get settled. Be good.

Dad

Exercise A: Leaving a Message
Part 1

At 7:15 on Monday morning, Mercedes gets a call from Lucky Grocery asking her to come for a job interview at 8:00 A.M. She should be able to get home by 10:00. She needs to leave right away, but Juanita is still asleep. Fill in the following message for Juanita.

day and time _____

Mama,

I went to _____

for _____.

I'll be back _____.

_____

Part 2

Now imagine that you have just been invited by your friend Rob to go bowling at Cherry Lanes. Your mother and brother, who live with you, are not home, and you are leaving right away. You won't be back until midnight. Leave them a message, giving them specific details.

WRITING INSTRUCTIONS

BRAINSTORMING

Brainstorming is a basic writing technique that will help you be sure that your reader "gets the message." It is a skill that you'll use many times in this exercise book.

The purpose of brainstorming is to get your thoughts flowing about your topic. To brainstorm, write down whatever ideas come to you that you might want to include when you write.

In the example that follows, Mercedes is brainstorming a list of tasks for Juanita and her children to work on while she is out being interviewed.

Example
Brainstorm

> Chores to Do
>
> pick up Paula's medicine
> wash dishes
> shovel front walk
> vacuum living room
> clean kids' bedrooms
> wash kitchen floor

Exercise B: Brainstorming for Instructions

In the space provided, write a brainstorm list for each situation.

1. You have a baby-sitter coming for the evening to care for your children. Brainstorm at least five items for a list of instructions to leave for the sitter.

2. You have been given a birthday gift from a friend. He is going to run errands for you all day Saturday, and he will do anything you ask him to do. Brainstorm at least four errands you need done.

3. Your sister is taking a woodworking class and wants to build you a bookcase. Brainstorm at least six things you would tell her to make sure you got the kind of bookcase you wanted.

See *Putting It in Paragraphs*, pages 41–43, for more on brainstorming.

Mercedes finished her brainstorming and looked back at her list. She decided she would pick up Paula's prescription herself, so she crossed that item off. Now she is ready to write the instructions, using the items she thought of when she brainstormed and adding some details to make them clearer.

ORDER OF IMPORTANCE

An easy way to let your reader know which items are most important is to put the important ones first. When Mercedes wrote her instructions, she put them in order of importance, as you can see in the following example.

Model

INSTRUCTIONS IN ORDER OF IMPORTANCE

2/12/90

Mama and children,
Here are some chores I want you to do after school. If you can't get everything done, the first ones are most important.

1. clean children's rooms (pick up, dust, sweep floors)

2. wash dishes—be sure to check throughout house for dirty dishes

3. shovel front walk (Ramon or Rita should do this)

4. wash kitchen floor (sweep, then mop)

5. vacuum living room

Thanks!
Mercedes

Exercise C: Writing Instructions in the Order of Importance

Go back to your three brainstorm lists from Exercise B. Choose <u>one</u> and use it to write instructions. Follow these steps to write your instructions:

1. Revise your brainstorm list by adding anything else you can think of or crossing out anything that doesn't really belong.
2. On a separate sheet of paper, rewrite your brainstorm list as a list of instructions, leaving space to write between each item and putting the items in order of importance.
3. Add any details your reader would need in order to understand what you mean by each item.
4. If you need to, copy your instructions on a separate sheet of paper so they can be read easily.

WRITING DIRECTIONS

SEQUENCE

Sequence refers to the time order of events. For example, you could use sequencing in your writing to tell someone how to get to a certain place. You would give directions in the order in which each turn should be taken. As you read through the following model, imagine what would happen if the directions were out of sequence!

Model

SEQUENCE OF STEPS

1. Take Highway 9 west from your building to LaGrange Road.
2. Turn right on LaGrange and go two miles.
3. At Route 58, turn left.
4. Take 58 about a mile until you see a huge town square on the right and places to park on the left. Park.
5. Meet me at the inn on the southeast corner of the square.

Exercise D: Writing Directions in Sequence

Below is a map showing the neighborhood where Mercedes and her family live.

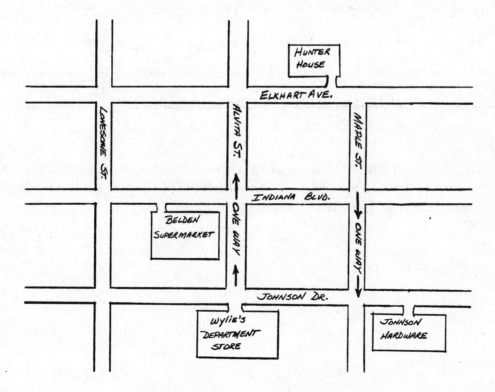

Part 1

Juanita needs to go to the supermarket, the hardware store, and Wylie's Department Store. Mercedes is planning her trip for her, and she wants to figure out the easiest way for Juanita to drive to those three places and home again. In the space below, write directions so that Juanita could not possibly get lost.

Part 2

Give the map on page 93 and your directions to another person. Have the person draw Juanita's route on the map. If the person can't follow your directions, rewrite them more clearly.

SEQUENCE IN OTHER SITUATIONS

Sequence is important in many situations. Imagine what would happen if someone gave you directions for changing a tire and told you to jack up the car after you took off the flat. You'd have a pretty hard time following those directions!

In the exercise that follows, be sure to think through exactly what order the steps should be in. Also be sure not to leave out any steps. Assume that your reader has no previous knowledge of the task.

Exercise E: Writing More Directions in Sequence

Choose two of the following situations and write directions for them. Before you write, brainstorm a preliminary list of the steps your reader will need. Then, write your final directions on a separate sheet of paper.

1. Your spouse never had a checking account before marrying you and needs to know how to use one. Using any checkbook and check record that is familiar to you, write directions for writing out and recording a check.

2. A friend has complimented you on one of your favorite dishes and wants to try to make it himself. You know he doesn't know a lot about cooking. Write very careful instructions to go along with your recipe.

3. You are going on a vacation. Select a task you perform frequently at work or at home and write directions so that someone can do it for you while you're gone.

4. Your mother recently discovered she could save money on gasoline by pumping it herself. She doesn't want to admit to the gas station attendant that she doesn't know how to pump gas, so she asks you to tell her how before she goes to the station. Write directions for her to follow.

Sample directions are on page 90.

CHAPTER 3

ANNOUNCEMENTS, NOTES, AND LETTERS

COVERING ALL THE FACTS IN A SHORT PARAGRAPH

Your writing does not need to be long to be effective. In fact, some of the most effective writing is short. Many people do not want to read long pieces of writing, so your reader is more likely to read your whole piece if it is short and to the point.

You can follow an easy formula when you have a simple message to get across. In this chapter, you'll practice writing announcements, notes, and letters by following the five Ws: WHO, WHAT, WHEN, WHERE, and WHY. You can cover the five Ws in one paragraph.

WHO can refer to you, your reader, or both you and your reader
WHAT the event you're writing about
WHEN the time the event occurred or will occur
WHERE the place or places involved
WHY can refer to your reason for writing, the reason for the event, or both

GUIDELINES FOR WRITING ANNOUNCEMENTS, NOTES, AND LETTERS

1. Get a mental picture of your reader and list the important facts you want to convey.
2. Choose the proper format for your writing. Are you writing an announcement, a note, or a letter?
3. Whenever possible, address your reader by name.
4. Check to be sure you included the five Ws.
5. Eliminate any information that is not necessary for your reader to understand your message and purpose.
6. Sign your name.

WRITING ANNOUNCEMENTS

In California, a friend of Paul's told him about an announcement of openings for crew managers at a big lettuce farm in the Salinas Valley. Paul, desperate for work, decided to apply. His experience in supervising work teams at the steel mill would come in handy. The announcement was posted at a community service center in Monterey. The handbill read:

Model

ANNOUNCEMENT

> ## JOB OPENINGS
>
> ## BUMPER CROP OF ICEBERG LETTUCE!
> ## GOLD STAR LETTUCE FARMS
> ### is taking applications for
> ## FARM WORK CREW LEADERS
> ### Saturday, April 21, 1990
> ### 2000 Valley Farm Road
> ### Salinas, California

Exercise A: Writing Announcements

Part 1

List the information in the model announcement above in the order of the five *W*s: who, what, when, where, and why.

1. WHO _____

2. WHAT _____

3. WHEN _____

4. WHERE _____

5. WHY _____

Answers are on page 90.

Part 2

Imagine you have realized your life's goal of opening your own business. Write an announcement telling your friends to come to an open house at your new business address to celebrate. Make up all the details you need. Fill in the chart below before you write to be sure you don't leave anything out.

WHO	
WHAT	
WHEN	
WHERE	
WHY	

WRITING NOTES

When Mercedes sent her mother a pair of huaraches for Christmas, Juanita was so glad to get them that she immediately wrote a thank-you note. Mercedes was relieved that her mother liked the shoes because they were so hard to find during the winter. Mercedes didn't expect her mother to be wearing them in northern Indiana in February, however!

Here's a copy of the thank-you note:

Model

**THANK-YOU
NOTE**

> 1450 Rio Grande Dr.
> San Antonio, Tx 78229
> December 30, 1989
>
> Dear Mercy,
>
> Thank you for the huaraches. They are very comfortable. Yesterday, I walked all over town with them on. I'll think of you whenever I wear them.
>
> Love,
> Mama

Exercise B: Writing a Thank-You Note

On a separate sheet of paper, write a short thank-you note thanking someone for a recent gift or favor. Or use this opportunity to thank someone whom you hadn't taken the chance to thank in the past. Use the model provided above as a guide.

WRITING A SHORT PERSONAL LETTER

The letter Mercedes wrote to her mother was short. The shock of Paul's leaving for California made writing a long letter painful.

Mercedes only wanted to inform her mother of the facts. She covered the five *W*s in one paragraph. She also followed the format for writing a personal letter: street address, city, state, zip code, and date in the upper right-hand corner; greeting, body of letter, closing followed by a comma, and signature.

Because of the mother/daughter relationship between Mercedes and Juanita, Mercedes wrote in an informal tone. Here is a copy of the letter she wrote:

Model

PERSONAL LETTER

> 9333 S. Elkhart Ave.
> Portage, In 47314
>
> February 2, 1990
>
> Dear Mama,
> How are you? I hope all is well. Paul left for California yesterday. I don't think he's coming back. He couldn't take being out of work. Sorry to trouble you with my problems, but I felt you should know. The kids are taking it as well as can be expected. Write when you can.
>
> Love,
> Mercy

Exercise C: Writing a Short Personal Letter

Part 1

Using the five *W*s shown in the chart below, write a one paragraph reply from Juanita to Mercedes. The letter should also express sympathy for Mercedes's situation. Use a separate sheet of paper.

WHO	Juanita
WHAT	is coming to Portage
WHEN	February 12, 1990
WHERE	arriving at Greyhound Bus Station
WHY	to help with the children

Part 2

Write a short personal letter to a friend or relative relating an important fact or event. Be sure to follow the form of a personal letter. Include the five *W*s.

In the space below, brainstorm what you will include in your letter. Then write your letter on a separate sheet of paper.

WRITING SHORT REQUEST LETTERS

When you write a short request letter, you are writing a business letter. You state clearly what you want from your reader. You include only the important facts the reader needs to understand the message. Two basic differences between a business letter and a personal letter are format and tone.

A business letter follows a format similar to that of a personal letter. However, above the greeting you put the address of the person you are writing to. Also, a colon instead of a comma follows the greeting.

The tone of a business letter is formal in contrast to the informal tone of a personal letter. Imagine how you would talk in a private conversation with a friend compared to how you would talk in a job interview. You would speak more formally in a job interview if you wanted to be taken seriously. A business letter, similarly, is written in a formal tone.

Mercedes noticed an ad in the daily newspaper for a free pamphlet on energy conservation. The pamphlet included simple tips for saving on utility bills and gasoline. With Paul gone, Mercedes felt she needed to learn as much as she could about weatherizing the house and taking care of the car. She wrote a letter to the agency:

9333 S. Elkhart Ave.
Portage, In 47314
February 14, 1990

S. James
Consumer Information Center
P.O. Box 100
Pueblo, Co 81002

Model

REQUEST LETTER

Dear Sir or Madam:

I would like to receive your free booklet about energy conservation. The booklet was advertised in the Sunday Times on February 11, 1990. It is called <u>Your Keys to Energy Efficiency</u>, 587N. Please mail the booklet to:

Mrs. Mercedes Hunter
9333 S. Elkhart Ave.
Portage, In 47314

Sincerely,
Mrs. Mercedes Hunter

Exercise D: Check Your Understanding

Compare the tone and format of the above letter with those of the personal letter from Mercedes to Juanita on page 25.

1. Why is the tone different in the two letters?

_____

_____

2. List at least two words or phrases from the request letter that give it a businesslike tone._____

3. What are the differences in format between the personal letter and the request letter?_____

4. Which of the five *W*s does the request letter include?

_____

Answers are on page 90.

Exercise E: Writing a Request Letter

Following the format shown in the model on page 27, write a letter to S. James, Consumer Information Center, P.O. Box 100, Pueblo, CO 81002, to request one of the following free booklets:

Plain Talk about Raising Children. 549N.
> Suggestions and advice from experienced parents.

A Woman's Guide to Social Security. 514N.
> What every woman should know about benefits upon retirement, disability, widowhood, or divorce.

Snack Facts. 505N.
> How snacking can harm your teeth; attractive chart of snack foods that are least likely to cause decay.

That Lite Stuff. 534N.
> FDA requirements for low-calorie, sugar-free, or diet foods.

Your Keys to Energy Efficiency. 587N.
> Tips for saving energy at home or in your car; health-related issues; state and local consumer and energy offices.

ADDRESSING AN ENVELOPE

An important step in writing a letter is addressing an envelope. A properly addressed envelope has two addresses: the return address, located in the upper left-hand corner of the envelope; and the mailing address, located in the center of the envelope. The return address includes the sender's name, street address, city, state, and zip code. The mailing address shows the receiver's title and name (if known), street address, city, state, and zip code.

Model

ENVELOPE

Mrs. Mercedes Hunter
9333 S. Elkhart Ave.
Portage, In 47314

S. James
Consumer Information Center
P.O. Box 100
Pueblo, Co 81002

Exercise F: Addressing an Envelope

Address an envelope for your letter, using the format above. Mail your letter. (Be sure to put postage on it.)

CHAPTER 4

GETTING YOUR MONEY'S WORTH

Few people can afford to throw their money away. As a consumer, you want to get full value from the food, clothing, housing, appliances, and services you buy.

When something goes wrong with an item or service you purchased, writing is a useful tool for getting your money's worth. In this chapter, you will learn to write a consumer complaint letter.

WHY WRITE A CONSUMER COMPLAINT LETTER?

Why is it a good idea to write a letter when you have a complaint about something you bought?

First of all, it gives both you and the seller a written record of your complaint. If your case were to go to a court or an agency such as the Better Business Bureau, your letter would be evidence of the problem. Second, you can ensure that the seller knows exactly what the problem is. Third, you can tell the seller exactly what you want done about the problem. In this chapter, you'll practice writing an effective consumer complaint letter by

- identifying the product or service
- stating your problem clearly
- including evidence for the problem
- stating the outcome you want as a result of your letter

Always keep a copy of your letters.

INCLUDING COMPLETE INFORMATION

Paul has recently moved into a small apartment in a large complex. The complex is owned and operated by Boxwood Management Company. The roof in his apartment leaks. He has had to move his clothes out of his bedroom closet to keep them dry. He has spoken to the resident manager about getting the roof repaired, but nothing has been done. He decides to put his complaint in writing to the management company.

Model
TENANT COMPLAINT LETTER

Paul Hunter
3421 N. Grove Ave., Apt. 5
Los Angeles, Ca 92106
March 12, 1990

Boxwood Management Company
1512 Dodge St.
Los Angeles, Ca 92112

Dear Madam or Sir:

On March 2, I discovered that the roof leaks in the bedroom of my apartment. I reported the problem the same day to the resident manager. He said the roof would be fixed the next day. However, the roof is still leaking. I have been forced to move my clothes out of the closet, where the leaking is worst. The closet ceiling looks ready to collapse. Please have my roof repaired immediately.

Sincerely,
Paul Hunter

Exercise A: Checking for Complete Information

Part 1

Using the information in the model above, answer the following questions in the spaces provided.

1. Where is the problem?_____

2. What is the problem?_____

3. What has Paul already done to try to get the problem solved?_____

_____

4. What evidence is there of the problem?_____

_____

5. What does Paul want the management company to do?_____

_____

Part 2

This part of the exercise is based on the following tenant complaint letter:

> *Paul Hunter*
> *3421 N. Grove Ave., Apt. 5*
> *Los Angeles, Ca 92106*
> *May 14, 1990*
>
> *Boxwood Management Company*
> *1512 Dodge St.*
> *Los Angeles, Ca 92112*
>
> *Dear Madam or Sir:*
>   *Some carpet in my apartment is mildewed. It smells and it is discolored. I talked to the resident manager about it, and he said I had to contact you. I want the carpet replaced as soon as possible.*
>
>   *Sincerely,*
>   *Paul Hunter*

Answer the following questions as completely as you can based on the letter above. If there is not enough information in the letter to answer a question, write *need more info* in the blank.

1. What problem is Paul telling the management company about?

_____

2. Which room or rooms is the problem in?_____

3. What caused the problem?_____

_____

4. What evidence is there of the problem?_____

_____

5. What does Paul want the management company to do about the

problem?_____

Answers are on page 90.

SELECTING DETAILS FOR A COMPLAINT LETTER

Since every problem is different, there's no perfect formula to tell you what details to include in a complaint letter. Ask yourself what your reader would need to know in order to solve your problem. It's a good idea to brainstorm details you might want to include before you write. (If you don't remember how to brainstorm, review pages 16–17.)

Rita, Mercedes's daughter, ordered a record from her record club. When it arrived, she found that it was scratched. She chose the following details to include in her letter to the record club.

Model

DETAILS FOR A COMPLAINT LETTER

> *When record came, could see scratch on side 1*
> *returning Street Talk by Peggy's Pursuit*
> *catalog number F-378*
> *send replacement*
> *scratch can be heard when record is played*

GUIDELINES FOR SELECTING DETAILS FOR A COMPLAINT LETTER
1. Identify the product or service.
2. State your problem clearly.
3. Include evidence of the problem.
4. State the outcome you want as a result of your letter.
5. Don't include irrelevant information.

Exercise B: Selecting Details for a Complaint Letter

When you complete each part of this exercise, be sure you keep your work. You will need it later.

Part 1

On March 9th, Mercedes took her '80 Volvo to M & M Transmission because the car wouldn't shift into reverse. She was promised that the car would be ready in two weeks. Instead, it took four weeks to fix it. The job cost $700. Two days later, her son Ramon drove it to work, and the car wouldn't shift into reverse. He had to circle the block to find a parking space he could pull into. This made him late for work, causing his boss to issue a warning.

M & M normally backs its work with a 2,000-mile guarantee. When Mercedes tried to make the garage honor the guarantee, the service manager said the guarantee didn't apply to foreign cars. Mercedes wants M & M to fix the car under the guarantee. She decides to complain in writing to the owner of the company.

1. In the space below, brainstorm a list of details Mercedes might include in her letter.

2. Using the guidelines on page 32, check over your list. Cross out anything that doesn't directly relate to the problem. Add anything you think will help her case or clarify the problem.

A list of details is on page 90.

Part 2

Now choose a situation in your own life you would like to write a complaint letter about. Perhaps you would like your landlord to fix something in your apartment. Maybe something you bought recently fell apart the first time you used it.

1. In the space below, brainstorm a list of at least five possible details you could include in your letter.

2. Using the guidelines on page 32, go over your brainstormed list. Cross out any irrelevant details. Add any others your reader might need.

PUTTING YOUR THOUGHTS IN ORDER

Now that you have finished selecting details for a letter, you're ready to put them in the order in which you want them to appear in the letter. Be sure your train of thought will make sense to your reader.

You can order your details in the same sequence as that given in the guidelines on page 32. Group the same types of details together. Here are the four guidelines that tell you the order:

1. Identify the product or service.
2. State your problem clearly.
3. Include evidence of the problem.
4. State the outcome you want as a result of your letter.

Exercise C: Putting Your Thoughts in Order

Part 1

Here are the details for Rita's letter to her record club. Number them in the order in which they might appear in her letter.

_____ when record came, could see scratch on side 1

_____ returning *Street Talk* by Peggy's Pursuit

_____ catalog number F-378

_____ send replacement

_____ scratch can be heard when record is played

Part 2

Number your list of details for Mercedes's letter to the owner of M & M Transmissions in the order they should appear. You made this list in Exercise B, Part 1.

Part 3

Now number your list of details for your letter about your own situation in the order they should appear. You made this list in Exercise B, Part 2.

Answers and an ordered list for Mercedes's letter are on page 90.

WRITING A CONSUMER COMPLAINT LETTER

A consumer complaint letter is a business letter. Look back at the model letter from Paul to Boxwood Management Company on page 30. Check for the following elements of a business letter:

- return address (the writer's name and address)
- inside address (the receiver's address)
- date
- greeting, followed by a colon (*Dear Madam or Sir:*)
- closing, followed by a comma (*Sincerely,*)

Now that you have selected the details for your letter, put them in order, and reviewed the elements of a business letter, you are ready to write. You just have to turn your details into complete sentences to create your letter. In the exercise that follows, refer to the model on page 30 if you need to.

Exercise D: Writing a Consumer Complaint Letter

Part 1

Write a complaint letter from Mercedes to the owner of M & M Transmissions. His name is Hank Ruzinsky. The address is 3648 E. Hobart St., Portage, IN 47316. Use your list of details from Exercise C, Part 2. Be sure to use business letter format.

On a separate sheet of paper, first write a rough draft of Mercedes's letter. Then write the final letter.

Part 2

Turn your list of details from Exercise C, Part 3, into a complaint letter. Be sure to use business letter format. On a separate sheet of paper, first write a rough draft of your letter. Refer back to the checklist on page 32 to make sure you have written an effective letter.

Then write your final letter. When you are finished, make a copy of your letter. Address an envelope for your letter (refer to page 28 if you need to review addressing an envelope). Mail your letter.

CHAPTER 5

WRITING FOR INFORMATION OR ADVICE

By writing a letter when you need information or advice, you can make sure that you communicate all the information your reader needs to answer your questions. In this chapter, you will learn to write a letter that will get you the answers you need.

In each exercise, you will be working on the same two pieces of writing, taking each one through the writing process. Be sure to keep your work from each exercise since you will need it later.

WHAT TO INCLUDE IN AN INFORMATION REQUEST LETTER

An information request letter is not hard to organize. You should include three main categories of details:

1.	**Background/Introduction**	your situation and your purpose for writing
2.	**Body**	the specific information you want
3.	**Request for response and closing**	where and by when to send information; thanks for assistance

Ramon, Mercedes's son, will graduate from high school at the end of May. In high school, he took a vocational course in auto mechanics and discovered that he has a knack for fixing cars. He decides to write to some training programs in auto mechanics that his guidance counselor recommends.

He decided to use the first two sections of the chart above as a guide for brainstorming details for his letter.

**Example
Brainstorming
for an
Information
Request Letter**

my situation and purpose for writing:
 —graduating from high school
 —high school auto mechanics teacher said I was good
 —interested in career in auto mechanics
 —checking out different programs

specific information I want:
 —requirements to get in
 —classes required to complete program
 —commuting time from home to school
 —cost and length of program
 —success in placing graduates in jobs

Exercise A: Brainstorming for an Information Request Letter

Brainstorm details for an information request letter for each of the following situations. Refer to the example and the chart as much as you need to.

1. Think of an educational program you might want to register for, such as a GED, community college, or vocational program. Brainstorm details for the letter you would write to get information about the program and the procedure for application and registration.

2. Think of a trip you have always wanted to take, such as visiting a national park, going on a whitewater rafting trip, or staying at a resort. Imagine that you are going to take your trip on your next vacation. Brainstorm details for the letter you would write to find out information for planning your trip.

OUTLINING AN INFORMATION REQUEST LETTER

Outlining is a way to organize the details you brainstorm for a letter and put them in the order you want. You wrote several short outlines in Chapter 4, Exercise C: Putting Your Thoughts in Order. Now you are working with more details that fall under several headings, so you will find it even more important to keep yourself organized by writing outlines.

When you outline, you group your brainstormed details under headings. At this point, you may decide that not all the details on your brainstormed list are appropriate or relevant. You may also think of new things and add them to your outline.

The outline for Ramon's letter looked like this:

Model

OUTLINE FOR INFORMATION REQUEST LETTER

1. Tell about myself and my purpose for writing
   —graduating
   —interested in career in auto mechanics
   —checking out different programs

2. Ask for information about the program
   —requirements to get in?
   —what classes required to complete program?
   —are classes during the day or at night?
   —cost and length of program?
   —success in placing graduates in jobs?

3. Say where and when to send information
   —need information in time to apply to program
   —send to my home address
   —thank for assistance

Exercise B: Check Your Understanding

Compare the example brainstorm for an information request letter on page 36 with the model outline for an information request letter on page 38. Answer the following questions.

1. What two details appear on the brainstormed lists but do not appear on the outline?_____

_____

2. Why do you think Ramon left these two details out when he wrote his outline? First detail:_____

Second detail:_____

3. What new detail appears in section 2 of the outline that did not appear on the brainstormed list?_____

4. Which part of the outline will be the body of the letter?

_____

5. Which part of the outline will be the introductory part of the letter?

_____

6. Which part of the outline will be the closing part of the letter?

_____

Answers are on page 90.

Exercise C: Outlining an Information Request Letter

Go back to the lists of details you brainstormed in Exercise A, page 37. Turn your brainstormed details into outlines. Remember that you don't have to use all the details from your brainstorm lists, and you can add new details. Refer to the chart on page 36 and the model on page 38 as much as you need to.

WRITING AN INTRODUCTORY PARAGRAPH

Ramon wrote the introductory paragraph of his letter based on section 1 of his outline. The first sentence of his paragraph would be the first sentence of his letter, so he knew it should state the purpose of the whole letter. Then he turned each of the details on his outline into sentences.

Ramon used a formal tone in writing his letter. An information request letter is a business letter. He also wanted to give a good impression since he might eventually want to be admitted to one of the programs he was writing to.

The model below shows Ramon's introductory paragraph. The first sentence is the **unifying statement** for the letter. It is in dark type.

Model

INTRODUCTORY PARAGRAPH FOR INFORMATION REQUEST LETTER

> **I would like some information about your program in auto mechanics.** I am graduating from high school in May, and I would like to begin a career in auto mechanics. Right now I am looking into several programs recommended by my guidance counselor.

Exercise D: Writing Introductory Paragraphs

Go back to the outlines you wrote in Exercise C. Write an introductory paragraph based on each one. Refer to the model as much as you need to. Keep in mind that your outline is only a guide. You can add new details or omit details from your outline when you write your paragraph.

Space is provided for you to write your paragraphs below and on the next page. You may want to use this space for rough drafts and write your final drafts on a separate sheet.

WRITING THE BODY PARAGRAPH

The core of Ramon's letters was his body paragraph. In this paragraph he told his readers exactly what information he needed.

He started by writing a **topic sentence** for the paragraph. A topic sentence summarizes what the paragraph is about. In the model below, the topic sentence is underlined. The other sentences are based on the details in Ramon's outline. Compare the model paragraph with section 2 of the outline on page 38.

Model

BODY PARAGRAPH FOR INFORMATION REQUEST LETTER

I have some specific questions about your program. What are the entrance requirements? What classes will I need to take to complete the program? Are the classes offered during the day or in the evening? What is the cost of the program, and how long is it? Also, what percentage of your students are you able to place in jobs when they complete the program?

Exercise E: Writing Body Paragraphs

Write body paragraphs for each of your letters, using the outlines you wrote in Exercise C, page 40. Refer to the model on page 42 as much as you need to. Remember, you can add or omit details. Your outline is only a guide.

Space is provided for you to write your paragraphs below and on the next page. You may want to use this space for rough drafts and write your final drafts on a separate sheet.

WRITING THE CONCLUDING PARAGRAPH

Ramon wanted to make sure that the places he wrote to understood how to satisfy his request. He wrote his concluding paragraph, making sure that his readers had all the necessary information.

Model

CONCLUDING PARAGRAPH FOR INFORMATION REQUEST LETTER

> Please send me this information within three weeks. My home address is 9333 S. Elkhart Ave., Portage, In 47314. In case you should need it, my home phone number is 219/591-0827. Thank you very much for your assistance.

Exercise F: Writing Concluding Paragraphs

Now write concluding paragraphs for your two information request letters based on your outline. Refer to the model as much as you need to. Remember, your outline is only a guide.

Space is provided for you to write your paragraphs below. You may want to use this space for rough drafts and write your final drafts on a separate sheet.

Exercise G: Completing an Information Request Letter

Choose <u>one</u> of your information request letter topics. On a separate sheet of paper, copy or type your paragraphs, putting them in business letter format. If you need to review business letter format, see page 30. Prepare an envelope and mail your letter.

CHAPTER 6

WRITING TO PERSUADE

When you write to persuade, your purpose is to convince your reader to agree with your point of view. You may also want your reader to take action.

Persuasive writing may take several forms in everyday life. A very common form of persuasive writing is advertising. After all, the purpose of an ad is to persuade you to take action—to buy the product. Another common form of persuasive writing is editorials. In an editorial, the editors of a newspaper or magazine express their opinion about an issue of interest to their readers.

However, not all persuasive writing is written by professionals. In Chapter 4, you learned to write complaint letters, one form of persuasive writing. And ordinary citizens often write letters to editors of newspapers and magazines and letters to politicians and other officials. You may also discover other purposes for persuasive writing throughout the chapter.

In this chapter, you will practice writing persuasive letters that are several paragraphs in length. You will work on:

- stating your opinion clearly
- using reasons that support your opinion
- summarizing your point of view

Throughout the chapter, you will be working toward writing persuasive letters of your own. Save your work from each exercise, since you will often use it in later exercises.

GETTING STARTED ON A PERSUASIVE LETTER

The first paragraph of your letter should begin with a unifying statement. A unifying statement for persuasive writing tells your reader:

- what the topic of your letter is
- what your opinion is

Rita, Mercedes's daughter, read an editorial in the *Portage Press*. It said the state of Indiana should stop providing Spanish translations of public information such as income tax instructions, occupational safety regulations, and public transit schedules. The editor thought that no one should be allowed to live in the United States who could not read this information in English. The editorial said the state was wasting money helping people who didn't belong.

Rita disagreed. She thought of her mother and grandmother, who had come from Mexico. She decided to write a letter to the editor in response to the editorial. She started by writing her unifying statement.

Model

> *The state of Indiana should continue to provide Spanish translations of important public information.*

Notice that Rita's statement makes both her topic and her opinion clear to her readers.

Exercise A: Identifying and Improving Unifying Statements

For each of the following sentences, write *OK* on the line below it if the sentence is a good unifying statement. If it is not a good unifying statement, rewrite it so that it 1) has a clear topic and 2) takes a position on the issue. You may have to make up new information to add to some sentences. The first one is done for you as an example.

1. Mr. Girard was right.

   Mr. Girard was right to make his grown son move out.

2. All drunken drivers should serve sentences in jail.

   _____

3. The Equal Rights Amendment is probably unnecessary.

   _____

4. Your garage must pay for the repairs my car needs.

   _____

5. Pollution may destroy the Baker Wildlife Preserve.

   _____

6. Public schools might be improved if taxes were raised.

   _____

7. President Allen has done the right thing.

   _____

8. Our main press is hazardous and must be replaced by May 1.

   _____

9. Ms. Shapere may not be the one for the job.

   _____

10. You must provide our building with more heat.

_____

Answers and rewritten sentences are on page 91.

Exercise B: Writing Unifying Statements

Imagine you are writing letters to the editor of your local paper. Write <u>five</u> unifying statements in which you make your topic and your opinion clear to your readers. Below are some general ideas for topics. You can also make up your own. Select issues that interest you. The first one is done for you as an example.

1. national health insurance (health insurance for everyone, paid for by the government)
   National health insurance is the simplest solution for rising health care costs.
2. teenage pregnancy
3. salaries in professional sports
4. possession of handguns
5. the nuclear arms race
6. a hazardous waste dump in your area
7. legalization of marijuana
8. reforms needed in the public schools

1. _____

   _____

2. _____

   _____

3. _____

   _____

4. _____

   _____

5. _____

   _____

For more information on unifying statements, see pages 14 and 18 of *Writing for a Purpose.*

SELECTING SUPPORTING REASONS

After you have introduced your topic with your unifying statement, your next step is to select reasons that will support your opinion and convince your reader. These supporting reasons are really the core of your persuasive letter.

Brainstorming is one way to begin thinking of reasons that support your position. See pages 16–17 to review brainstorming.

GUIDELINES FOR SELECTING SUPPORTING REASONS

1. Be sure your reasons actually say something new. Don't just restate your opinion.
2. Be sure your reasons actually support your point of view. Don't include something just because it relates to the topic.

Rita wrote the following list of reasons she would use to support her unifying statement (shown in the model on page 47).

Model

SUPPORTING REASONS FOR PERSUASIVE LETTER

> *Unifying Statement: The state of Indiana should continue to provide Spanish translations of important public information.*
>
> *Supporting Reasons:*
>
> 1. *Money spent to assist Spanish-speaking people is an investment in members of our community.*
> 2. *Spanish-speaking immigrants might not be able to find the resources they need to get started in the U.S.*
> 3. *It takes people several years to learn a new language, and they need assistance while they are learning.*
> 4. *Depriving Spanish-speaking people of information after they've already come to the U.S. will not make them go back to their native countries.*
> 5. *People who do not speak English could place themselves and others in danger in some situations.*

Use this model and the guidelines above to help you in Exercises C and D.

Exercise C: Identifying Supporting Reasons

Below are a unifying statement and a list of sentences. Read the unifying statement carefully. Put an **X** in the blank next to the sentences that would make good supporting reasons. You may have to compare each supporting reason with the unifying statement.

Unifying Statement: Legislation is still needed to make sure women are treated fairly by employers.

_____1. More women than ever before are members of the work force.

_____2. Women still earn less than men who perform the same jobs.

_____3. Women are still excluded from jobs that traditionally have been held by men.

_____4. It took an amendment to the constitution to affirm racial equality.

_____5. Studies have compared many aspects of different jobs and found that men are paid more than women for comparable jobs.

_____6. Many women are responsible for housework and child care in addition to their job responsibilities.

_____7. Employers claim that they can't afford to pay women more.

_____8. The government should make sure that women are paid what they are worth.

_____9. Women are less likely than men to be promoted to higher-paying supervisory positions.

Answers are on page 91.

Exercise D: Writing Supporting Reasons

Select two of your unifying statements from Exercise B, page 48. In the spaces below, write down at least three supporting reasons for each one. Refer to the guidelines and the model on page 49 to check your work. Your supporting reasons do not have to be complete sentences. Just be sure you will be able to understand your notes later.

For more information on supporting reasons, see pages 74-76 of *Writing for a Purpose.*

WRITING A CONCLUDING STATEMENT

Now that Rita has taken a position in her unifying statement and found reasons to support it, she is ready to summarize her point of view. Her concluding statement firmly restates the position she introduced in her unifying statement. It will add the final "punch" to her letter.

Model

CONCLUDING STATEMENT FOR PERSUASIVE LETTER

> *The state of Indiana is acting in its own best interests by providing Spanish translations of public information.*

Exercise E: Writing Concluding Statements

In the spaces below write concluding statements for the same unifying statements you selected to work with in Exercise D, page 51. Be sure that your concluding statements restate your position clearly.

_____

_____

_____

_____

For more information on writing concluding statements, see pages 15-16 and 26 of *Writing for a Purpose*.

OUTLINING A PERSUASIVE LETTER

Rita has already developed most of her letter. She has a unifying statement, four supporting reasons, and a concluding statement. Now all she has to do is make sure she has it organized in such a way that she can write it up easily.

PARTS OF A PERSUASIVE LETTER

opening paragraph	—begins with unifying statement —contains another sentence or two of introduction

body of letter	—contains supporting reasons
	—may be more than one paragraph
	—each reason can be developed into its own paragraph
	    or reasons may be grouped into paragraphs
	    or reasons may be listed in one paragraph

concluding paragraph	—begins with concluding statement —may close with another sentence or two

Rita based the outline of her letter on the chart above. She decided to write four paragraphs. The organization of her material is shown in the outline on the next page.

Model

OUTLINE OF A PERSUASIVE LETTER

1. Introductory paragraph
   —state should continue to provide translations
   —as a Hispanic, I don't agree with editorial

2. Assisting Spanish speakers = investment in people
   —helps immigrants find resources needed to get settled
   —public safety—of Spanish speakers and others

3. Translations are not real issue
   —Hispanics are here to stay
   —different languages are part of life in a diverse nation
   —real issue is making diversity work for everyone

4. Concluding statement
   —the state of Indiana is acting in its own best interests

Exercise F: Check Your Understanding

Compare sections 2 and 3 of Rita's outline shown in the model above with her list of supporting reasons shown in the model on page 49. Answer the following questions.

1. What did she leave out of her outline?

   _____

2. What did she add to her outline?

   _____

3. Which of the supporting reasons will be topic sentences for her body paragraphs?

   _____

Answers are on page 91.

Exercise G: Outlining a Persuasive Letter

Outline two persuasive letters based on your work in Exercises B, D, and E. Be sure to organize your supporting reasons carefully. You can also omit or add supporting reasons at this point.

For more information on organizing ideas, see pages 19-23 of *Writing for a Purpose*.

PUTTING IT ALL TOGETHER

At this point, Rita is ready to write her letter. In the model below, you will see that she followed her outline fairly closely. However, at this stage many writers find that they want to make changes. For example, Rita developed a concluding paragraph when she wrote her letter, adding an idea she hadn't thought of when she wrote her outline. When you read the concluding paragraph, find the idea that she added.

Model

LETTER TO THE EDITOR

> 9333 S. Elkhart Ave.
> Portage, IN 47314
> March 30, 1990
>
> Letters to the Editor
> Portage Press
> 3100 East Portage Dr.
> Portage, IN 47310
>
> To the Editor:
>   The state of Indiana should continue to provide Spanish translations of important public information. As a Hispanic, I cannot agree with your editorial. My experience with my own family and our community gives me a different point of view.
>   Money spent to assist Spanish-speaking people is an investment in members of our own community. Spanish-speaking immigrants need translated information in order to find the resources they need to get started right in the U.S. In addition, Spanish-speaking people could place themselves and others in danger in some situations if warning signs and safety information are not translated for them.
>   Depriving people of information after they are already in the U.S. doesn't address the real issue raised in the editorial. Hispanic people will surely continue to come to the United States. Different languages are part of life in a diverse nation. The real issue before us is the challenge of making diversity work for all of us.
>   The state of Indiana is acting in its own best interests by providing Spanish translations of public information. Perhaps the editors of the Portage Press should look back into their own family histories. They might find that their own families have not always spoken English.
>
>   Sincerely,
>   *Rita Hunter*
>   Rita Hunter

Exercise H: Writing a Letter to the Editor

Part 1

When Hoosier Steel Works closed, shifting its production overseas, the *Portage Press* printed an editorial criticizing the action. The paper accused the corporation of acting irresponsibly. The newspaper received a flood of letters both for and against its editorial.

Supporting reasons for two different letters are given below. You can also use supporting reasons that you think of yourself. Write a letter to the editor representing one point of view. Outline your letter before you write. The address of the paper is 3100 East Portage Dr., Portage, IN 46310.

If you agree with the *Portage Press's* editorial accusing Hoosier Steel of acting irresponsibly—

Reasons supporting your position:

1. plant's closing left thousands of Indianans unemployed
2. northern Indiana's economy has been seriously hurt
3. retail stores were forced to close
4. moving operations overseas is harmful to American workers
5. Hoosier Steel shouldn't desert the town that made it successful

If you disagree with the editorial accusing Hoosier Steel Works of acting irresponsibly—

Reasons supporting your position:

1. the steel union's wage demands were too high
2. Hoosier Steel Works helped the town's economy for 50 years and owes it nothing
3. Hoosier Steel's first responsibility is to its stockholders
4. Hoosier Steel could no longer make a profit here
5. town should have seen this coming and should have developed other economic plans

Part 2

In Exercise G you did most of the work on writing two letters to the editor on topics of your own choice. Now choose <u>one</u> of those letters to finish. Write it carefully in business letter format, addressing it to your local newspaper.

Make sure your letter has the following features:

- a unifying statement that makes your topic and opinion clear
- supporting reasons that add new evidence to your argument
- a concluding statement that summarizes your argument

Prepare an envelope and mail your letter. You might just see your name in print!

Part 3

When politicians decide how to cast their votes in Congress, one factor they consider is the number of letters they have received in favor of or opposing an issue. They know they need to represent the voters who elected them.

You can write to your U.S. congresspersons at these addresses:

The Honorable _____ (name of your senator)
United States Senate
Washington, DC 20510

The Honorable _____ (name of your represenative)
United States House of Representatives
Washington, DC 20515

There are a number of ways you can find out who your U.S. senators and representatives are if you don't know. Perhaps the easiest way is to call your public library. A librarian will be able to help you based on the information on your voter registration card. You can also call your local chapter of the League of Women Voters.

Choose a subject that you feel Congress should do something about. If you can't think of anything, scan the newspaper, watch the evening news, or ask your friends what they think of the latest news from Washington.

After you have chosen a topic, follow these steps and write a letter to your congressperson defending your point of view. Your letter will be answered, and you will find out what your congressperson's point of view on the issue is.

1. Write a unifying statement in the space below.

_____

_____

_____

2. In the space below, brainstorm and select supporting reasons.

3. Write a concluding statement in the space below.

_____

_____

_____

4. Outline your letter in the space below.

5. Write your letter on a separate sheet of paper, prepare an envelope, and mail it.

CHAPTER 7

GETTING A JOB

USING DIFFERENT TYPES OF WRITING

As you have already seen in this book, writing takes different forms, depending on your purpose. Finding a job is a purpose that requires several different types of writing, such as filling out forms and writing resumes, thank-you letters, and cover letters. You have studied similar writing tasks in earlier chapters in this book. In this chapter, you will be putting these writing tasks to work for the purpose of a job search.

JOB APPLICATION FORMS

A job application form is very important because it represents you to the employer, and you want to make a good impression.

GUIDELINES FOR FILLING OUT EMPLOYMENT APPLICATION FORMS

(For general guidelines on filling out forms, review page 6.)

1. Before you go to apply for a job, gather the information that you are likely to need, such as exact addresses, telephone numbers, and names of your former employers and three personal references. Write them down on a piece of paper and take them along.
2. Fill out the application very neatly.
3. Do your best to fill out the form on your own. Asking too many questions may indicate to the employer that you have trouble working independently. However, asking a question is better than making a mistake.

In the *Los Angeles Times*, Paul saw ads for two job openings that interested him. One firm, Sun State Electronics, was looking for parts assemblers. The other company, Digitron Computers, was looking for quality control supervisors. Paul decided to apply to Sun State Electronics because the ad said to apply in person. The other ad said to send a resume to apply, and Paul didn't have one.

Exercise A: Filling Out a Job Application Form

Using the facts below, complete the application form for Paul by filling in the spaces. Remember that Paul has worked for only one company in his life.

date can start: April 2, 1990   salary desired: $20,000
grammar school: Trewell Heights Elementary, Trewell Heights, IN
high school: Anderson High School, Portage, IN; graduated
former employer: Hoosier Steel Works, 2692 Linnon Dr., Portage, IN 47322
supervisor: J.D. Reid   former salary: $30,000
reference: Walter Duggan, 590 Yellow Cove Rd., Portage, IN 47304,
hardware store owner, acquainted 20 years
notify in emergency: Mercedes Hunter, 9333 S. Elkhart Ave., Portage, IN 47314, 219/555-0827

APPLICATION FOR EMPLOYMENT
(PRE-EMPLOYMENT QUESTIONNAIRE)   (AN EQUAL OPPORTUNITY EMPLOYER)

PERSONAL INFORMATION

DATE _____

SOCIAL SECURITY
NUMBER _____

NAME _____
      LAST   FIRST   MIDDLE

PRESENT ADDRESS _____
      STREET   CITY   STATE

PERMANENT ADDRESS _____
      STREET   CITY   STATE

PHONE NO. _____   ARE YOU 18 YEARS OR OLDER   Yes ☐   No ☐

SPECIAL QUESTIONS

DO NOT ANSWER **ANY** OF THE QUESTIONS IN THIS FRAMED AREA UNLESS THE EMPLOYER HAS **CHECKED** A **BOX PRECEDING** A QUESTION, THEREBY INDICATING THAT THE INFORMATION IS REQUIRED FOR A BONA FIDE OCCUPATIONAL QUALIFICATION, OR DICTATED BY NATIONAL SECURITY LAWS, OR IS NEEDED FOR OTHER LEGALLY PERMISSIBLE REASONS.

☐ Height _____ feet _____ inches

☐ Weight _____ lbs.

☐ What Foreign Languages do you speak fluently? _____   Read _____   Write _____

☐ _____

☐ Citizen of U.S. ____ Yes ____ No

☐ Date of Birth* _____

*The Age Discrimination in Employment Act of 1967 prohibits discrimination on the basis of age with respect to individuals who are at least 40 but less than 70 years of age.

EMPLOYMENT DESIRED

POSITION _____   DATE YOU CAN START _____   SALARY DESIRED _____

ARE YOU EMPLOYED NOW? _____   IF SO MAY WE INQUIRE OF YOUR PRESENT EMPLOYER? _____

EVER APPLIED TO THIS COMPANY BEFORE? _____   WHERE? _____   WHEN? _____

EDUCATION	NAME AND LOCATION OF SCHOOL	*NO. OF YEARS ATTENDED	*DID YOU GRADUATE?	SUBJECTS STUDIED
GRAMMAR SCHOOL				
HIGH SCHOOL				
COLLEGE				
TRADE, BUSINESS OR CORRESPONDENCE SCHOOL				

*The Age Discrimination in Employment Act of 1967 prohibits discrimination on the basis of age with respect to individuals who are at least 40 but less than 70 years of age.

GENERAL

SUBJECTS OF SPECIAL STUDY OR RESEARCH WORK

U.S. MILITARY OR NAVAL SERVICE _____   RANK _____   PRESENT MEMBERSHIP IN NATIONAL GUARD OR RESERVES _____

TOPS FORM 3285 (REVISED)   (CONTINUED ON OTHER SIDE)   LITHO IN U.S.A.

LAST   FIRST   MIDDLE

FORMER EMPLOYERS [LIST BELOW LAST FOUR EMPLOYERS, STARTING WITH LAST ONE FIRST].

DATE MONTH AND YEAR		NAME AND ADDRESS OF EMPLOYER	SALARY	POSITION	REASON FOR LEAVING
FROM					
TO					
FROM					
TO					
FROM					
TO					
FROM					
TO					

REFERENCES: GIVE THE NAMES OF THREE PERSONS NOT RELATED TO YOU, WHOM YOU HAVE KNOWN AT LEAST ONE YEAR.

	NAME	ADDRESS	BUSINESS	YEARS ACQUAINTED
1				
2				
3				

PHYSICAL RECORD:

DO YOU HAVE ANY PHYSICAL LIMITATIONS THAT PRECLUDE YOU FROM PERFORMING ANY WORK FOR WHICH YOU ARE BEING CONSIDERED?   □ Yes   □ No

PLEASE DESCRIBE:

IN CASE OF EMERGENCY NOTIFY

NAME   ADDRESS   PHONE NO.

"I CERTIFY THAT THE FACTS CONTAINED IN THIS APPLICATION ARE TRUE AND COMPLETE TO THE BEST OF MY KNOWLEDGE AND UNDERSTAND THAT, IF EMPLOYED, FALSIFIED STATEMENTS ON THIS APPLICATION SHALL BE GROUNDS FOR DISMISSAL.

I AUTHORIZE INVESTIGATION OF ALL STATEMENTS CONTAINED HEREIN AND THE REFERENCES LISTED ABOVE TO GIVE YOU ANY AND ALL INFORMATION CONCERNING MY PREVIOUS EMPLOYMENT AND ANY PERTINENT INFORMATION THEY MAY HAVE, PERSONAL OR OTHERWISE, AND RELEASE ALL PARTIES FROM ALL LIABILITY FOR ANY DAMAGE THAT MAY RESULT FROM FURNISHING SAME TO YOU.

I UNDERSTAND AND AGREE THAT, IF HIRED, MY EMPLOYMENT IS FOR NO DEFINITE PERIOD AND MAY, REGARDLESS OF THE DATE OF PAYMENT OF MY WAGES AND SALARY, BE TERMINATED AT ANY TIME WITHOUT ANY PRIOR NOTICE."

DATE   SIGNATURE

DO NOT WRITE BELOW THIS LINE

INTERVIEWED BY   DATE

HIRED: □ Yes   □ No   POSITION   DEPT.

SALARY/WAGE   DATE REPORTING TO WORK

APPROVED: 1.   2.   3.

EMPLOYMENT MANAGER   DEPT. HEAD   GENERAL MANAGER

This form has been designed to strictly comply with State and Federal fair employment practice laws prohibiting employment discrimination. This Application for Employment Form is sold for general use throughout the United States. TOPS assumes no responsibility for the inclusion in said form of any questions which, when asked by the Employer of the Job Applicant, may violate State and/or Federal Law.

WRITING A THANK-YOU LETTER FOR AN INTERVIEW

It is a good practice to follow up an employment interview with a thank-you letter. A letter keeps your name in the mind of the interviewer and is another chance to persuade the company to hire you.

GUIDELINES FOR WRITING A THANK-YOU LETTER FOR A JOB INTERVIEW

1. Follow the format for a business letter.
2. Begin by thanking the person for the interview.
3. State specific reasons why you want to work for the company and why you would make a good employee.
4. End by thanking the interviewer again.

Mercedes applied for a job as a bookkeeper for the Centertown Clinic. Mercedes had worked as a bookkeeper before her children were born, and she had kept up her skills by managing the family's finances. After the interview, Mercedes wrote a thank-you letter. She followed the guidelines listed above.

Model

THANK-YOU LETTER FOR JOB INTERVIEW

9333 S. Elkhart Ave.
Portage, IN 47314
February 12, 1990

Ms. Mary Osterworth
Administrative Manager
Centertown Clinic
1825 N. Broad St.
Portage, IN 47305

Dear Ms. Osterworth:
    Thank you for considering me for the job as bookkeeper for Centertown Clinic. I enjoyed meeting and talking with you. Centertown Clinic has a good reputation in Portage, and I would be proud to join your staff.
    I am glad you are looking for a person who cares about patients as well as figures. For that reason, I feel that I would do the job well and would enjoy it very much. I am skilled in all areas of bookkeeping, but I care a lot about people. I also think my Spanish would be helpful with Centertown's Hispanic patients.
    Again, thank you for interviewing me for the job. I look forward to hearing from you soon.

Sincerely,
Mercedes Hunter
Mercedes Hunter

Exercise B: Check Your Understanding

1. List three reasons why Mercedes feels she should get the job.

   _____

   _____

2. What does Mercedes say that is complimentary to her prospective employer?

   _____

Exercise C: Writing a Thank-You Letter for an Interview

Using what you have learned about writing thank-you letters, write a thank-you letter from Paul Hunter, thanking Sun State Electronics for interviewing him for a job as parts assembler.

Here is the information you need for the letter:

Sun State Electronics
8000 El Camino Rd.
Los Altos, CA 92115
Interviewer's name: Mr. Preston Morgan

In your thank-you letter, include reasons why Paul should be hired for the job. Mention Paul's past experience as a line worker and foreman for Hoosier Steel Works. He has a good work record and has shown that he is quick and reliable. You can also mention that Paul is interested in the electronics industry because it is growing and has a future.

Use the space below to outline Paul's thank-you letter. Write the letter or a separate sheet of paper. (You will probably need to write a rough draft first.)

WRITING A RESUME AND COVER LETTER

Mercedes had seen several ads in the paper she was interested in but hadn't applied for because they said "send resume." So her next writing project was a resume.

WHAT IS A RESUME?

A resume is simply a summary of a person's work history and qualifications. Most resumes follow a similar format, although there is no single right way to do a resume. Your goal in writing a resume is to present yourself truthfully in the best possible way so that the employer will want to interview you in person.

WHAT TO INCLUDE ON A RESUME

A resume may contain any or all of the following information:

Possible Categories:	Might Include:
PERSONAL DATA	name, address, phone numbers
POSITION DESIRED	type of job you want, what field or industry you want to work in
WORK HISTORY	names and addresses of previous employers, dates of employment, job title, responsibilities, accomplishments
RELATED EXPERIENCE	volunteer work, homemaking, etc.
EDUCATION	degrees or highest year of schooling completed, any special training, any high school equivalency classes or degrees

GUIDELINES FOR WRITING A RESUME

1. Make your resume flawless. It should be perfectly typed and photocopied on clean plain stationery. Have someone else proofread it.
2. If you want to use the same resume to apply for several jobs, make it flexible. For example, you may not want to include the category Position Desired on your resume unless you are applying for only one type of job.
3. Use active words to describe your previous jobs, related experience, and education, such as *organized, completed, supervised, assisted, participated,* etc.
4. If you have not worked steadily, or you do not want to include all your jobs on your resume, do not include any dates.
5. Don't include unrelated information on your resume. Stick to facts that prove your ability to do the job or jobs you're applying for.

Mercedes worked on her resume for several hours, revising it several times. Finally she was ready to go to the public library, where she could type for $1 an hour on rental typewriters. She took paper and correcting fluid with her. Here is her finished resume:

Model

RESUME

Mercedes Hunter
9333 S. Elkhart Ave.
Portage, IN 47314
219/591-0827

POSITION DESIRED: Bookkeeper

WORK HISTORY:
   Bookkeeping Supervisor, Henrietta's Clothing Outlet.
   Responsible for all bookkeeping procedures at large
   clothing store. Supervised two assistants; advised store
   manager in financial matters.
   Bookkeeper, Eye Care Optometrists. Maintained all
   financial records; prepared tax information; reduced bad
   debt write-off on patient accounts by 40 percent.
   Accounts Receivable Clerk, Tadwell Community College.
   Kept records of student accounts.

RELATED EXPERIENCE:
   Manage finances for five-person household, including
   budgeting, banking, mortgage, and taxes.

EDUCATION:
   Tadwell Community College. Completed six semester-
   hours of basic accounting.
   Grant Memorial High School. Received high school
   diploma.

Exercise D: Check Your Understanding

To answer the following questions, compare Mercedes's resume above with the chart and guidelines on page 63.

1. List four active words Mercedes used to describe her experience and education:_____

2. Why do you think Mercedes did not include dates of employment on her resume?_____

3. What educational background does Mercedes have for the type of job she wants?_____

4. Should Mercedes use this resume to apply for a job as a sales clerk in a clothing store? ____ yes ____ no
   Give two reasons for your answer._____

Exercise E: Writing a Resume

Select a help wanted ad in your newspaper that you would like to respond to. Using the chart, guidelines, and model on pages 63–64 to refer to, compose a resume for yourself that would interest the employer in you. If you are actually going to use your resume to apply for a job, it should be typed.

Use the spaces below to make notes on what you will include on your resume. Then, on separate sheets of paper, write at least one rough draft before you write your final version.

Personal Data: _____

_____

_____

_____

Position Desired: _____

Work History: _____

_____

_____

_____

_____

_____

_____

_____

Related Experience: _____

_____

_____

Education: _____

_____

_____

WHAT IS A COVER LETTER?

You "cover" your resume with a cover letter to introduce yourself in writing to a prospective employer. Again, your purpose is to interest the employer in you so that you will get an interview. Your cover letter should not be long—about three short paragraphs will do the job in most cases.

WHAT TO INCLUDE IN A COVER LETTER

The following chart shows a way to organize the information you might want to include in a cover letter.

Opening paragraph	—where you heard about the job —why you are applying
Body paragraph	—summarize your most important qualifications for the job
Closing paragraph	—you hope to hear from employer soon —close with courteous thanks

GUIDELINES FOR WRITING A COVER LETTER

1. Your cover letter should be in business letter format.
2. It should be typed on plain business paper and proofread carefully by another person. Always send an original cover letter, not a photocopy.
3. Use your cover letter to emphasize the high points of your resume.
4. Tailor your cover letter to fit the job you're applying for. Say why you would be a good person for that particular job.

Mercedes wanted to respond to the following ad in the *Portage Press:*

BOOKKEEPER
Must be experienced in payroll, accounts receivable, accounts payable, and bank reconciliations. Send resume to: Holbrook and Sons, 521 Commercial Hwy., Portage IN 47302.

The following model shows the cover letter she wrote to send along with her resume on page 64.

Model

COVER LETTER

9333 S. Elkhart Ave.
Portage, IN 47314
February 8, 1990

Holbrook and Sons
521 Commercial Hwy.
Portage, IN 47302

Dear Madam or Sir:

    I am sending you my resume in response to your ad for a bookkeeper in the <u>Portage Press</u>. I have six years of experience as a bookkeeper, and I am fully qualified for the position.

    As you can see from my resume, I have been responsible for all aspects of bookkeeping for two different businesses, including payroll, accounts receivable, accounts payable, and bank reconciliations. I like working with people, but I am also very detail-oriented.

    I hope to hear from you very soon. Please feel free to call me at 555-0827 at any time to set up an interview. Thank you for your consideration.

               Sincerely,

               Mercedes Hunter

               Mercedes Hunter

Exercise F: Writing a Cover Letter

Write your own cover letter to go with your resume. Remember to tailor the cover letter to the specific requirements mentioned in the ad you are responding to in Exercise E. Refer to the chart, guidelines, and model on pages 66–67. (Turn to page 68 for writing steps for this exercise.)

Use the following writing steps as you organize and write your letter:

1. In the space below, brainstorm details to include.

2. In the space below, outline your letter in sections for each paragraph.

3. Write a rough draft of your letter on a separate sheet of paper. Make as many changes and corrections as you want on your rough draft.

4. Neatly copy or type your letter so that you have a perfect copy. If you are actually going to send your letter, it should be typed.

WRITING A LETTER OF INTRODUCTION

Many job openings are never advertised in the help wanted ads. How do you approach a prospective employer when you have no ad to go by?

One approach is writing a letter of introduction to the employer. A letter of introduction is very much like a cover letter. You usually enclose your resume with it.

WHAT TO INCLUDE IN A LETTER OF INTRODUCTION

Read through the following chart showing what you might include in a letter of introduction. Compare it with the chart for a cover letter on page 66.

Opening paragraph	—why you are writing to this employer —type of job you are looking for
Body paragraph	—summarize your most important qualifications
Closing paragraph	—request an interview —day and time you will call —close with courteous thanks

Mercedes began calling all her friends to tell them she was looking for work. Sheila, who worked in a warehouse for a supermarket chain, said there might be an opening for a bookkeeper there. She told Mercedes to contact Mr. Parker at SuperGrocer. Mercedes revised her cover letter into a letter of introduction.

After you read through the model below, compare it to the model cover letter on page 67. What differences do you notice?

Model

LETTER OF INTRODUCTION

> 9333 S. Elkhart Ave.
> Portage, IN 47314
> Feb. 8, 1990
>
> Mr. Parker
> SuperGrocer Warehouse
> 843 22nd St.
> Portage, IN 47302
>
> Dear Mr. Parker:
>   I am looking for a job as a bookkeeper. I have six years of experience, and I am a responsible and dedicated employee. My friend Sheila Pitt, who works at SuperGrocer, gave me your name and suggested I contact you.
>   As you can see from my resume, I have been responsible for all aspects of bookkeeping for two different businesses, including payroll, accounts receivable, accounts payable, bank reconciliations, and tax preparation. And at Henrietta's Clothing Outlet, I trained and supervised my assistants as well. I like working with people, but I am also very detail-oriented.
>   I would like to talk to you about job opportunities at SuperGrocer. I will call you on the 17th, a week from today, to make an appointment. Thank you for your consideration.
>
>   Sincerely,
>   *Mercedes Hunter*
>   Mercedes Hunter

Exercise G: Writing a Letter of Introduction

Go back to your cover letter, which you wrote in Exercise F on pages 67–68. Imagine a friend has told you about a possible job opening where he works. Make some notes to yourself about how you would rewrite your cover letter as a letter of introduction. Write your letter of introduction.

WRITING ON THE JOB

COMMUNICATION AT WORK

How many times have you heard someone at work say, "Could you write all that down?" or "Put that in writing for me, and I'll get it taken care of"?

Writing is one way to make sure that plans get carried out right, that everyone understands a policy, that people follow safety rules, or that people know what their jobs are. In this chapter, you'll practice the kinds of writing that many people use on the job.

MEMO FORM

Memos are a simple form that many people use on the job. A memo has some standard features that let the reader know important information about the memo. These features are shown in the model on page 72.

GUIDELINES FOR WRITING A MEMO
1. Follow memo format, using these headings above the message:
   To:
   From:
   Subject:
   Date:
2. Use your full name followed by your initials.
3. Use the full name of the person or specify the group of people the memo is directed to.
4. Make the specific subject of the memo clear in the heading.
5. Organize your thoughts carefully before writing your memo. Be sure to include only relevant information. Be sure you give your reader everything he or she needs to know.
6. State the purpose of your memo in the first sentence.
7. After you write your memo, check it carefully to be sure it is clear, organized, and complete. Rewrite it if necessary.

Mercedes ran into a problem in her new job at SuperGrocer. She wanted to make sure her new boss understood why her work was behind schedule, and she wanted to put her explanation in writing. She used memo format to write a short report to her boss. She kept a copy of her memo in case any problems came up later.

Model

MEMO

MEMO

To: Don Parker
From: Mercedes Hunter *MH*
Subject: Lateness of February Bank Reconciliation
Date: March 14, 1990

This memo should explain why I am behind schedule in completing the February bank reconciliation.

The February statement from the First Mercantile Bank does not reconcile with our books. Apparently several errors were made when our deposits were recorded in our books. As a result, the bank statement shows a balance that is $3,532.31 less than the amount shown on our books.

I understand that the bank reconciliation is to be completed by the fifteenth of each month under normal circumstances. However, I will not be able to finish it until the errors have been corrected and the books for February brought up to date. I am certain that the reconciliation will be finished by March 20. Please see me if you have any questions.

Exercise A: Check Your Understanding

1. What is the purpose of Mercedes's memo?

_____

2. Why is the bank reconciliation going to be late?

_____

3. By when is the bank reconciliation ordinarily to be done?

_____

4. By when will Mercedes have it finished?

_____

Answers are on page 91.

Exercise B: Writing a Memo From Notes

Mercedes's boss, Don Parker, was promoted, leaving his job as bookkeeping supervisor vacant. Mercedes felt qualified for his old job and decided to ask for the promotion. Below are some notes she jotted down. From these notes, write a memo from Mercedes requesting that she be considered for the job. Refer to the model and guidelines on page 71–72. Space is provided for you to outline the memo before you write.

4/11/90

to Mr. Michael Chin, Chief Financial Officer
subj. Position of Bookkeeping Supervisor

experience as supervisor
loyal and responsible
like working at SuperGrocer
experience in all aspects of bookkeeping
college study in accounting
ready for a bigger job
have proven myself already here

Exercise C: Writing a Memo

Now imagine that you need to take a three-month leave of absence from your job because your father is very ill and you must go help your family. You want your job to be waiting for you when you return. Write a memo to your supervisor requesting the leave of absence. Tell him or her the reasons why you should be allowed to take the leave and how you think your job could be covered while you are gone.

In the spaces below, brainstorm details to include and make an outline.

Now, write a rough draft of your memo on a separate sheet of paper. When you are finished writing, reread your memo. If you were your supervisor, would you think that you had presented convincing reasons and provided a good solution to the problem? Would you want to grant the leave? Find at least two ways you could strengthen your memo and write your final version.

MEETINGS AND MINUTES

A meeting is usually not worth the time it took unless you have a written record of the decisions that were made, projects that were planned, tasks that were delegated for follow-up, etc. Meeting records are called *minutes*. Minutes are a summary of the important things to remember from a meeting.

TAKING NOTES
GUIDELINES FOR TAKING NOTES FOR MEETING MINUTES
1. Write down the names of the people at the meeting.
2. Note the major points made in reports given at the meeting.
3. Write down the important points of discussion.
4. Write the exact wording of any resolutions or motions.
5. Carefully record the results of any votes.
6. Note all plans and suggestions for the future, including the names of people working on projects and the dates that their work is to be completed.
7. Note the date, time, and location of the next meeting.

You have to be fast when you're taking notes because people can talk a lot faster than you can write. The important thing is to take good notes that you can write up later. While you're taking notes, don't worry about spelling, grammar, complete sentences, or punctuation. Abbreviate anything you can to save time.

Exercise D: Practice Taking Notes

Part 1

Set aside about fifteen minutes. Call up a friend or relative whom you've been meaning to get together with. Strike up a conversation about what's happening in your life and then make a date to get together. Throughout the conversation, take notes about the major points you and the other person bring up about your lives and your plans for the future. Also be sure to write down all the specifics about your date. Space is provided below.

Part 2

Now choose a half-hour television show that you're familiar with. Sit down with paper and pencil and take notes as you watch. Make sure to note any important things the characters say and any important events. Keep a list of the products advertised during the commercials. Take notes on the previews of the next week's show, if there are any.

WRITING MINUTES

Once you have your notes to work from, your next task is to write up minutes that will serve as a record for everyone who was at the meeting. There's no one way to do this. You just need to be sure that the minutes will be understandable, useful, and complete.

Mercedes took the following notes at the weekly meeting of the bookkeeping staff at SuperGrocer. Don Parker presented some information about computerization and answered questions from the staff.

Example
Notes From a Meeting

4/2/90

present: Don, Sally, Rose, Ben, Mercedes, Bill, Danita

report, Don Parker:
computer accting should be in place 6/90
more efficient means can handle more work
no one will be laid off
paychecks will come a day sooner

Sally: what new work?
Don: warehouse will expand, financial reports will come out monthly

Merc: will we work on terminals instead of paper?
Don: yes, eventually—for a while will do both until sure system works

Danita: can we have input into choosing software?
Don: yes, one bookkeeper will work with me and Chin—anyone who wants to should talk to me privately before Mon.; we'll choose then

next mtg: Tues 4/10 8:30 A.M., Danita bringing doughnuts

She wrote up the minutes of the meeting for everyone. Compare the model below with the notes on page 76.

Compare the model below with the notes on page 76.

Model

MINUTES OF A MEETING

Meeting of the Bookkeeping Staff
April 2, 1990

Present: Don Parker, Sally Rutzky, Rose Kendall, Ben Marchiano, Mercedes Hunter, Bill Cumming, Danita Smith

Report from Don Parker on Computerized Accounting:

A computerized accounting system should be in place by June 1990. The system will make our department more efficient, so we will be able to handle more work than we can now. No one will be laid off as a result of the increased efficiency, but the department will be doing more.

Questions from the Staff:

Sally asked what new work the department would be taking on. Don explained that the warehouse will be expanding, creating a heavier workload. Also, financial reports will come out monthly instead of quarterly.

Mercedes asked if we will work on terminals instead of on paper. Don said that at first we will do both until we're sure the system works. Later, everything will be done on terminals.

Danita asked if we can have input into choosing software. Don said that one bookkeeper will be chosen to work with him and Michael Chin. Anyone who would like that job should speak to Don privately by Monday. He and Michael will choose from the volunteers.

Next Meeting: Tuesday, April 10, 8:30 A.M.

Submitted by Mercedes Hunter

Exercise E: Writing Minutes from Notes

The following week, Bill took notes at the bookkeeping department's meeting. Using his notes, write minutes for the meeting. In your minutes, include only important information or points of discussion that people need to remember. Write a rough draft in the space provided. Then write your final version on a separate sheet of paper.

Don—Danita chosen to help research software
thanked her for doughnuts

Mercedes—need to discuss bad check problem
two returned in one month from Janus
bank charges a lot
several other accounts bounced checks
may need stricter policy
makes a lot of work for us

Ben—maybe charge higher fines

Don—policy change has to come from Chin

Sally—can we tell him the problem?

Mercedes—higher fines might not help
problem customers should have to pay with certified checks

Don—will discuss with Chin by next meeting

next mtg: Tues. 4/10

Exercise F: Writing up Your Own Notes

Choose <u>one</u> of your sets of notes from Exercise D, either from your phone conversation or from the television show. Write a summary of the most important information in your notes. If you are writing about the television show, imagine that you are writing the summary for a person who could not see the show. If you are writing about your telephone conversation, imagine you are describing the conversation in a letter to another friend.

GRIEVANCES AND VIOLATION REPORTS

Sometimes employers, either accidentally or on purpose, do things that are unfair, unsafe, or illegal that affect their employees. In these situations, you may want to take action by writing a letter to your employer or to an outside agency.

For example, you may feel that you have been denied a promotion because of your race. Or perhaps you are aware that safety, health, or other legal regulations are being broken.

Sometimes you may not want to go to your employer with a problem. In that case, there may be a government agency that can help you. You can find out where to send your letter by visiting the public library. Ask a reference librarian for assistance.

The chart below gives you information about three major employment-related government agencies: the Occupational Safety and Health Administration (OSHA), the National Labor Relations Board (NLRB), and the Equal Employment Opportunity Commission (EEOC).

	Kinds of Grievances	How to Contact	Agency's Response
OSHA	Safety and health hazards in the workplace	Contact OSHA Area Office (under U.S. Dept. of Labor in phone book).	Inspects workplace; investigates accidents. May penalize employer.
EEOC	Discrimination based on race, sex, national origin, or age (protects workers 40–70)	In phone book	Schedules interview to evaluate complaint. Will investigate if they feel discrimination has taken place.
NLRB	Unfair labor practices; complaints related to union activities. Excludes government, agricultural and domestic workers.	In phone book	Investigates case. May reinstate employees who lose jobs because of unfair labor practices or get them back pay.

GUIDELINES FOR REPORTING A GRIEVANCE OR VIOLATION
1. Follow business letter format.
2. State the facts. Give as many specifics as possible, including names, dates, and exact events or details of conversations.
3. Write in a businesslike tone. Avoid exaggerating or making accusations you don't have specific evidence for.

Mercedes's friend Sheila, who works in the meat department at Super-Grocer, was locked inside a walk-in refrigerator for several hours because the inside latch was broken. The maintenance man made a temporary latch, saying a new permanent latch would be installed soon. Several weeks went by. When Sheila asked about the new latch, she was told that the temporary one was working fine and there was no need to spend the money on a new one.

When Sheila told Mercedes about the situation, Mercedes suggested writing a letter to the Occupational Safety and Health Administration (OSHA). She had seen some information about the agency on a poster near the time clock. From the poster, they got the address. They spent an hour working on the letter.

Model

REPORT OF SAFETY VIOLATION

Sheila Pitt
530 W. Moracca St.
Portage, IN 47312
April 10, 1990

U.S. Dept. of Labor OSHA
46 E. Ohio St., Room 422
Indianapolis, IN 46204

Dear Madam or Sir:

I'm writing to report an unsafe situation at the SuperGrocer warehouse where I work. The warehouse is located at 843 22nd St., Portage, IN 47302.

For several hours on March 17, I was locked in our meat refrigerator because the inside latch was broken. Our maintenance man rigged up a temporary latch until a new latch could be installed.

On April 7, I asked my supervisor when the new latch would be installed. He said that the temporary latch was working fine and there was no need to replace it.

I don't believe the temporary latch is safe. It is not strong enough for such a heavy door, and it is not attached firmly. I'm afraid there will be another accident. Please send a safety inspector to the warehouse. Thank you very much.

Sincerely,
Sheila Pitt

Exercise G: Check Your Understanding

1. What is the purpose of Sheila's letter?

_____

2. When was Sheila locked in the refrigerator?

_____

3. Why hasn't the temporary latch been replaced?

_____

4. What does OSHA stand for?

_____

5. What does Sheila want OSHA to do?

_____

Exercise H: Writing a report of a Health Violation

Write a letter to your city Department of Health based on the following situation. Get the address to write to from the city government listings in your phone book or from the public library. Refer to the guidelines on page 80 and the model on page 81. Space is provided for you to outline your letter.

According to a poster of health regulations in the restaurant where you work, if meat is left unrefrigerated for more than three hours, it cannot be served. You know that frequently the lunch cook, who goes home at 3:00, leaves out hamburger patties that he brought out during the noon rush. The dinner cook is often still using those patties until the dinner rush begins around 5:30. You have spoken to the manager, but she does not believe there is a problem.

CHAPTER 9

CHOOSING KEY WORDS FOR SHORT MESSAGES

In this exercise book, you have seen how writing tasks can progress from simple to complex—from sentences to paragraphs to more than one paragraph.

The length of what you write does not always reflect the difficulty you may have had in writing it, however. Sometimes a writing task requiring the fewest words can be the hardest to write.

Writing concisely pays off, particularly when you must pay for the number of words you use! Two writing tasks that depend on your ability to choose essential words are writing classified ads and writing telegrams.

WRITING CLASSIFIED ADS

You place a classified ad in a newspaper or magazine because you want to

- sell an item or property
- purchase an item or property
- fill a job opening
- offer a service

Writing a classified ad is similar to writing an announcement. You use some of the same elements of the five *W*s described in Chapter 3.

WHAT	WHAT is the subject of your ad. It comes first. WHAT includes particulars such as the description of the job being offered or description of the property for sale. WHAT sometimes indicates the salary or the price.
WHO	WHO is the name of the person or company offering or looking for the product, service, or job.
WHERE	WHERE usually includes the address or telephone number of the seller or provider of services.
WHEN	If WHEN is included as part of the ad, it tells the prospective buyer or applicant when to inquire.

GUIDELINES FOR WRITING CLASSIFIED ADS

1. Be specific about what you have to sell.
2. Put the item or service for sale at the beginning of the ad.
3. Describe the product or service so that it will appeal to a buyer.
4. Tell the potential buyer whom to contact and how.
5. Be concise—most ads charge per line.
6. If you want to use abbreviations, call the newspaper or magazine and ask how to abbreviate the words you want to use.

Ramon's hobby is working on cars. He has learned how to troubleshoot and correct many of the mechanical problems of the family's old Volvo Because of the car's condition, Mercedes suggested selling it. With the money obtained from the sale of the Volvo, she plans to make a down payment on a newer car. She asked Ramon to put an ad in the newspaper. Ramon composed the following ad:

Model

CLASSIFIED AD

> '80 Volvo 240DL, excellent condition, AM/FM stereo, automatic, new transmission. $2,000 or best offer. Ramon 591-0827 after 8 P.M.

Exercise A: Check Your Understanding

Answer the following questions based on the model above.

1. What is the subject of the ad?_____

2. List four things the ad tells you about the car._____

_____

3. Whom is the prospective buyer to contact?_____

_____

Answers are on page 91.

Exercise B: Writing a Classified Ad Based on Information

Using the information in the paragraph below, write a classified ad for Juanita. Space is provided for your rough draft. Follow the guidelines and model above. If you want to see more examples of classified ads, look in your local newspaper.

Juanita Esperanza loves children. She has a lot of time on her hands during the day. Mercedes suggested that she baby-sit for working mothers in the neighborhood. Mercedes said that she could operate the service out of their home. She helped her mother obtain a license to baby-sit. Juanita plans to charge $50 per week. She will accept children 6 months old and older.

_____

_____

_____

_____

Exercise C: Writing Your Own Classified Ad

Write a classified ad in which you offer for sale some special item of yours. Be sure to follow the guidelines on page 84. Call your local newspaper to find out if you can abbreviate some of the words you want to use. Space is provided for your rough draft.

_____

_____

_____

_____

WRITING TELEGRAMS

The telegram is probably the best example of concise writing. A telegram is a message transmitted by wire over a distance. You are charged for each word in a telegram. Therefore, you use only the words necessary to get the message across, often writing in phrases or sentence fragments that make your message sound like a code.

GUIDELINES FOR SENDING A TELEGRAM
1. Write out the complete message you want to communicate.
2. Rewrite the message in as few words as possible without losing any essential information.
3. Reread the shortened message to make sure it conveys the information.
4. Sign your name.
5. Take the message to the nearest Western Union station.

Exercise C: Reducing Information to a Telegram

Write telegrams using as few words as necessary to communicate in the situations below. Assume that you will be charged $17.70 for ten words or less and $.45 for each additional word. Your goal is to save as much money as you can without losing the important facts.

Part 1

Paul was hired by Sun State Electronics at his desired salary. He was told that, depending on his performance, he could advance to supervisor in a year's time.

Finally finding a job with promise changed Paul's outlook on life. Although he had deserted the family, he missed them and wanted them in California with him. He planned to send Mercedes a telegram to share his excitement about the new job and to tell her that he would be coming to Indiana in a month to take the family back with him to California. In his telegram, he would tell her to start packing.

Write a telegram from Paul to Mercedes.

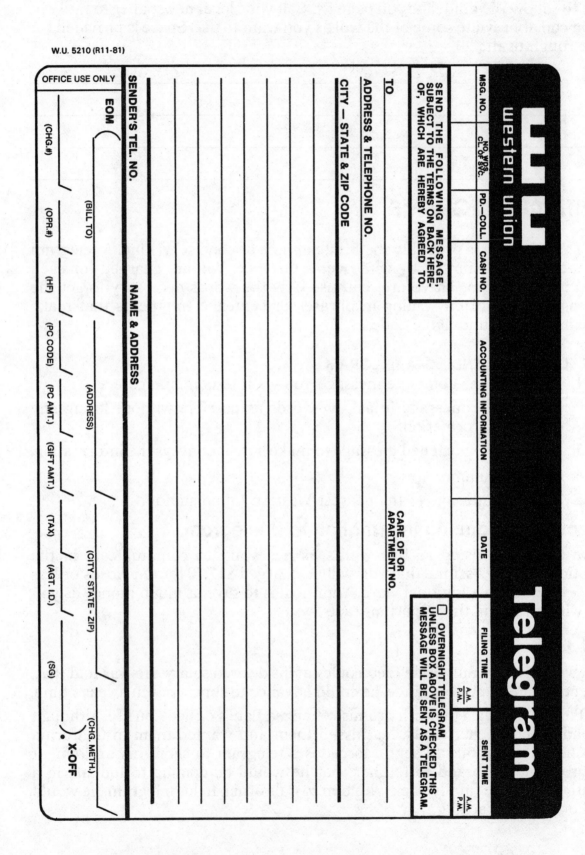

W.U. 5210 (R11-81)

A possible telegram from Paul is on page 91.

Part 2

Write a telegram from Mercedes responding to Paul's telegram. Follow the same guidelines as you followed in the exercise above. This is an opportunity for you to supply your own ending for the Hunter family story.

CHAPTER 1

Exercise A

1. She had no cash to deposit.
2.
```
   313.83   total of checks
 − 30.00   cash received
  283.83   net deposit
```
3. She would write them on the back of the deposit slip.

Exercise D

AFFIDAVIT OF REGISTRATION— DECLARACIÓN JURADA DE EMPADRONAMIENTO

STATE OF—ESTADO DE CALIFORNIA
COUNTY OF—CONDADO DE
LOS ANGELES

PRINT IN INK—ESCRIBA EN LETRA DE MOLDE EN TINTA

1 Optional · Opcional— ☒ Mr/Sr ☐ Mrs/Sra ☐ Miss/Srta ☐ Ms
Name · Nombre (first · nombre) (middle · segundo) (last · apellido)
Paul   Hunter

2 Residence · Domicilio (No.) (Street · Calle) (Apt. No. · Núm. del Apt.)
3421 N. Grove #5

3 City · Ciudad   **4** Zip Code · Zona Postal
Los Angeles   92106

5 Describe location of residence: (cross streets, section, township, range)
Describa la localidad de su residencia: (Calles que atraviesan, etc.)
Intersection of Grove Ave. and Dodge St.

6 Mailing Address (if different) · Dirección Postal (si diferente) (Rte or Box)

City · Ciudad   Zip Code · Zona Postal

7 Political Party · Partido Político (Check One · Indique uno)
☐ American Independent ☒ Democratic
☐ Republican ☐ Peace and Freedom
☐ Other · Otro ____ ☐ Decline to State · Se niega a declarar

8 Date of Birth
Fecha de nacimiento
mo. · mes / day · día / yr · año
12 / 21 / 46

9 State or Country of Birth
Estado o país de nacimiento
ILLINOIS

10 Occupation · Profesión u Oficio
Unemployed

11 Telephone (Optional)
Teléfono (Opcional)
813/555-0075

12 Social Security No. (Optional)
Núm. de seguro social (Opcional)
123-45-6789
☐ I prefer election materials in English
☐ Prefiero materiales electorales en español

13 Signature · Firma
Paul Hunter

WARNING: Perjury is punishable by imprisonment in State prison of not less than 1 nor more than 14 yrs. § 126 Penal Code, 2015.5 Civil Proc.

I am a citizen of the United States and will be at least 18 years of age at the time of the next election. I am not imprisoned or on parole for the conviction of a felony which disqualifies me from voting. I certify under penalty of perjury that the information on this affidavit is true and correct.

AVISO—El juramento en falso es castigable con encarcelamiento en la prisión del estado por no menos de uno y no más de catorce años. § 126 Penal Code, 2015.5 Civ. Proc.

Soy ciudadano de los Estados Unidos y tendré por lo menos 18 años de edad para la próxima elección. No estoy preso, o bajo el régimen de libertad provisional por un crimen que me prive del derecho de votar. Juro bajo pena de falso juramento que la información en esta Declaración Jurada es verdadera y correcta.

Date · Fecha
4-10-90

14 Signature person assisting (if any) · Firma, persona que ayuda (Si hubiera)
Subscribed in County of · Firmada en Condado de
Los Angeles

15 ☐ I will require assistance at the polls
☐ Yo necesito ayuda en la caseta de votación

NAME AS PREVIOUSLY REGISTERED · NOMBRE COMO PREVIAMENTE EMPADRONADO

PRIOR REGISTRATION PORTION: PORCIÓN DE EMPADRONAMIENTO PREVIO: ☒ NO
ARE YOU CURRENTLY REGISTERED TO VOTE IN CALIFORNIA? ☐ YES · Sí
¿ESTA UD. EMPADRONADO PARA VOTAR ACTUALMENTE EN CALIFORNIA?
(if YES, fill in below · Si afirmativo, llene los espacios abajo)

Former Address · Dirección Anterior:

City · Ciudad   County · Condado

Political Party – Partido Político

Office Use

ZA 726149

19**90** Form W-4

Department of the Treasury
Internal Revenue Service

Purpose. Complete Form W-4 so that your employer can withhold the correct amount of Federal income tax from your pay.

Exemption From Withholding. Read line 6 of the certificate below to see if you can claim exempt status. *If exempt, complete line 6; but do not complete lines 4 and 5.* No Federal income tax will be withheld from your pay. This exemption expires February 15, 1991.

Basic Instructions. Employees who are not exempt should complete the Personal Allowances Worksheet. Additional worksheets are provided on page 2 for employees to adjust their withholding allowances based on itemized deductions, adjustments to income, or two-earner/two-job situations. Complete all worksheets that apply to your situation. The worksheets will help you figure the number of withholding allowances you are

entitled to claim. However, you may claim fewer allowances than this.

Head of Household. Generally, you may claim head of household filing status on your tax return only if you are unmarried and pay more than 50% of the costs of keeping up a home for yourself and your dependent(s) or other qualifying individuals.

Nonwage Income. If you have a large amount of nonwage income, such as interest or dividends, you should consider making estimated tax payments using Form 1040-ES. Otherwise, you may find that you owe additional tax at the end of the year.

Two-Earner/Two-Jobs. If you have a working spouse or more than one job, figure the total number of allowances you are entitled to claim on all jobs using worksheets from only one Form

W-4. This total should be divided among all jobs. Your withholding will usually be most accurate when all allowances are claimed on the W-4 filed for the highest paying job and zero allowances are claimed for the others.

Advance Earned Income Credit. If you are eligible for this credit, you can receive it added to your paycheck throughout the year. For details, obtain Form W-5 from your employer.

Check Your Withholding. After your W-4 takes effect, you can use **Publication 919**, Is My Withholding Correct for 1990?, to see how the dollar amount you are having withheld compares to your estimated total annual tax. Call 1-800-424-3676 (in Hawaii and Alaska, check your local telephone directory) to order this publication. Check your local telephone directory for the IRS assistance number if you need further help.

Personal Allowances Worksheet

A Enter "1" for **yourself** if no one else can claim you as a dependent . . . . **A** `1`

B Enter "1" if:
  1. You are single and have only one job; or
  2. You are married, have only one job, and your spouse does not work; or
  3. Your wages from a second job or your spouse's wages (or the total of both) are $2,500 or less. . . . . **B** `1`

C Enter "1" for your **spouse.** But, you may choose to enter "0" if you are married and have either a working spouse or more than one job (this may help you avoid having too little tax withheld) . . . . **C** ___

D Enter number of **dependents** (other than your spouse or yourself) whom you will claim on your tax return . . . **D** `1`

E Enter "1" if you will file as a **head of household** on your tax return (see conditions under "Head of Household," above) . . **E** `1`

F Enter "1" if you have at least $1,500 of **child or dependent care expenses** for which you plan to claim a credit . . . . . **F** `1`

G Add lines A through F and enter total here . . . . ▶ **G** `5`

For accuracy, do all worksheets that apply.
- If you plan to **itemize or claim adjustments to income** and want to reduce your withholding, turn to the Deductions and Adjustments Worksheet on page 2.
- If you are **single** and have **more than one job** and your combined earnings from all jobs exceed $25,000 OR if you are **married** and have a **working spouse or more than one job,** and the combined earnings from all jobs exceed $44,000, then turn to the Two-Earner/Two-Job Worksheet on page 2 if you want to avoid having too little tax withheld.
- If **neither** of the above situations applies to you, **stop here** and enter the number from line G on line 4 of Form W-4 below.

------------------------ Cut here and give the certificate to your employer. Keep the top portion for your records. ------------------------

Form **W-4**	**Employee's Withholding Allowance Certificate**	OMB No. 1545-0010
Department of the Treasury Internal Revenue Service	▶ **For Privacy Act and Paperwork Reduction Act Notice, see reverse.**	19**90**

1 Type or print your first name and middle initial ___ Last name
CYNTHIA J.   LAUBER

2 Your social security number
123-45-6789

Home address (number and street or rural route)
469 OAKDALE

City or town, state, and ZIP code
MIDDLEBURY, COLORADO 88887

3 Marital status
☒ Single ☐ Married
☐ Married, but withhold at higher Single rate.
Note: *If married, but legally separated, or spouse is a nonresident alien, check the Single box.*

4 Total number of allowances you are claiming (from line G above or from the Worksheets on back if they apply) . . . **4** `5`

5 Additional amount, if any, you want deducted from each pay . . . . **5** $ ___

6 I claim exemption from withholding and I certify that I meet **ALL** of the following conditions for exemption:
- Last year I had a right to a refund of **ALL** Federal income tax withheld because I had **NO** tax liability; **AND**
- This year I expect a refund of **ALL** Federal income tax withheld because I expect to have **NO** tax liability; **AND**
- This year if my income exceeds $500 and includes nonwage income, another person cannot claim me as a dependent.

If you meet all of the above conditions, enter the year effective and "EXEMPT" here . . . . ▶ **6** | 19 ___

7 Are you a full-time student? (**Note:** *Full-time students are not automatically exempt.*) . . . . **7** ☐ Yes ☐ No

Under penalties of perjury, I certify that I am entitled to the number of withholding allowances claimed on this certificate or entitled to claim exempt status.

Employee's signature ▶ *Cynthia J. Lauber*   Date ▶ Jan. 25 , 19 90

8 Employer's name and address (**Employer:** Complete 8 and 10 **only if sending to IRS**)

9 Office code (optional)

10 Employer identification number

CHAPTER 2

Exercise E

2. Heat four cups of water in a large pot. When the water starts to boil, toss in a tablespoon of salt. Then add half of a one-pound package of spaghetti. Cook over a low flame. After around eight minutes, take a piece of spaghetti out of the pot and throw it against the kitchen wall. If the piece sticks, the spaghetti is ready. Drain it in a colander. Serve with butter and salt.

CHAPTER 3

Exercise A

Part 1

1. Gold Star Lettuce Farms
2. taking applications for farm work crew leaders
3. Saturday, April 21, 1990
4. 2000 Valley Farm Road, Salinas, California
5. bumper crop of iceberg lettuce

Exercise D

1. The letter from Mercedes to Juanita has an informal tone because the women have a personal relationship. Mercedes's letter to S. James is more formal because it is a business letter.
2. "Dear Sir or Madam"/"Sincerely"
3. The business letter has the address of the person Mercedes is sending the letter to. In the personal letter, there is a comma after the greeting rather than a colon.
4. who, what, where, and when

CHAPTER 4

Exercise A

Part 1

1. In the roof above the bedroom of Paul's apartment
2. The roof leaks.
3. He reported the problem to the resident manager of his apartment.
4. His clothes were getting wet. The closet ceiling looks like it's going to collapse.
5. He wants the company to have the roof repaired immediately.

Part 2

1. some mildewed carpet in his apartment
2. need more info
3. need more info
4. The carpet smells and it is discolored.
5. He wants the company to replace the carpet.

Exercise B

Part 1

Took the car to M & M Transmission on March 9
Car ('75 Volvo) wouldn't shift into reverse
Two days after being fixed, car wouldn't shift into reverse
Work done on the car cost $700
M & M advertises 2,000-mile guarantee, but service manager says the guarantee doesn't apply to foreign cars
Garage should fix the car again without charging her
No one ever told Mercedes that the guarantee didn't apply to her

Exercise C

Part 1

3—when record came, could see scratch on side 1
1—returning *Street Talk* by Peggy's Pursuit
2—catalog number F-378
5—send replacement
4—scratch can be heard when record is played

Part 2

2—Took the car to M & M Transmission on March 9
1—Car ('75 Volvo) wouldn't shift into reverse
4—Two days after being fixed, car wouldn't shift into reverse
3—Work done on the car cost $700
5—M & M advertises 2,000-mile guarantee, but service manager says the guarantee doesn't apply to foreign cars
7—Garage should fix the car again without charging her
6—No one ever told Mercedes that the guarantee didn't apply to her

CHAPTER 5

Exercise B

1. high school mechanics teacher said I was good, commuting time from home to school
2. First detail: Ramon doesn't need to give this detail in order to get the right information. Second detail: He can figure out the commuting time himself when he knows where the school is and how he will get there.
3. Are classes during the day or at night?
4. the second part
5. the first part
6. the third part

CHAPTER 6

Exercise A

2. OK
3. Since there are many laws that support women's rights, the Equal Rights Amendment is unnecessary.
4. OK
5. Pollution will destroy the Baker Wildlife Preserve if we don't stop Corman Chemical Co. from dumping its waste there.
6. Public schools will be able to hire more teachers if taxes are raised.
7. President Allen has done the right thing in proposing a new plan to balance the budget.
8. OK
9. Ms. Shapere is definitely not the one for the job.
10. OK

Exercise C

Good supporting reasons: 2, 3, 5, 7, 9

Exercise F

1. It takes people several years to learn a new language, and they need assistance while they are learning.
2. Translations not the real issue; different languages are part of life in diverse nation; real issue is making diversity work for everyone
3. Assisting Spanish speakers = investment in people; translations are not the real issue

CHAPTER 7

Exercise B

1. She cares about patients, speaks Spanish, and is skilled in all areas of bookkeeping.
3. She says that she enjoyed meeting and talking with her and would be proud to join her staff.

Exercise D

1. You should have chosen four of the following: responsible, supervised, advised, maintained, prepared, reduced, kept (records), managed, completed, received.
2. She doesn't want to highlight the fact that she has been out of the work force for a long time.
3. She has completed six semester hours of basic accounting.
4. No. This resume emphasizes her bookkeeping skills and states that she wants a position as a bookkeeper.

CHAPTER 8

Exercise A

1. to explain why she's behind schedule in completing the February bank reconciliation
2. The bank statement doesn't reconcile with their books.
3. by the fifteenth of each month
4. by March 20

Exercise G

1. to report an unsafe situation at her workplace
2. on March 17
3. Sheila's supervisor says the temporary latch on the refrigerator door is safe.
4. Occupational Safety and Health Administration
5. send a safety inspector to the SuperGrocer warehouse

CHAPTER 9

Exercise A

1. '80 Volvo for sale
2. It's in excellent condition, has an AM/FM stereo, is an automatic (not stick shift), and has a new transmission.
3. Ramon

Exercise C

Part 1

Found great job. Will come next month, bring you and kids here. Start packing!

Paul

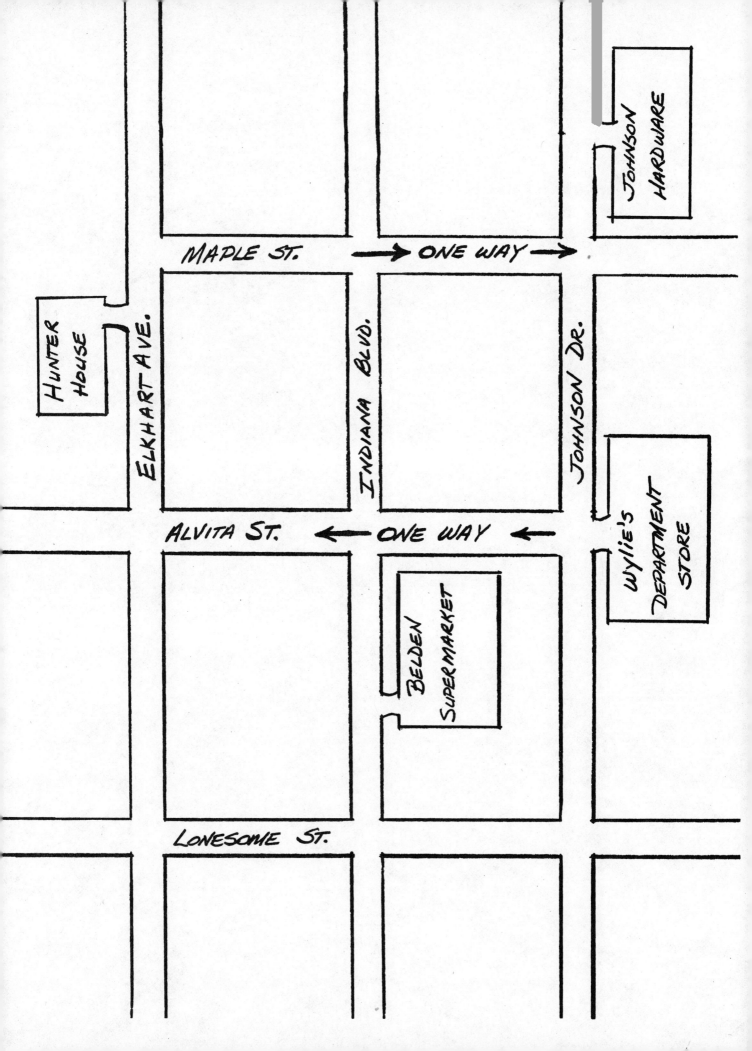